24/1

RANDY HERBERT

ISBN 978-1-0980-8562-9 (paperback)
ISBN 978-1-0980-8563-6 (digital)

Christian Faith Publishing, Inc.
832 Park Avenue
Meadville, PA 16335
www.christianfaithpublishing.com

The views expressed in this book are those of the author and do not necessarily reflect the official policy and position of the Department of Defense or the US Government. The public release clearance of this publication by the Department of Defense does not imply Department of Defense or US Government endorsement or factual accuracy of the material.

Printed in the United States of America

This book is dedicated to all the men and women in the military serving our country and working for the men and women beside them, those who are still with us as well as all those who died in the line of duty namely, 2nd Lt. Darryn Andrews, thirty-four, from Dallas, Texas, killed in an attack with an improvised explosive device and a rocket-propelled grenade, survived by his wife, Julie, and two-year-old son. The couple also have a daughter who was born three months after Andrew's death.

SSgt. Clayton Bowen, twenty-nine, from San Antonio, Texas, killed when an improvised explosive device discharged near his vehicle, survived by his mother and stepfather.

SSgt. Kurt Curtiss, twenty-seven, from Salt Lake City, Utah, killed by small-arms fire during an enemy attack, survived by his wife, Elizabeth, nine-year-old son, and six-year-old daughter.

PFC Matthew Michael Martinek, twenty, from Dekalb, Illinois, killed in an attack with an improvised explosive device and a rocket-propelled grenade, survived by his father, mother, and two brothers.

SSgt. Michael Murphrey, twenty-five, from Snyder, Texas, killed in an attack with an improvised explosive device, survived by his wife, Ashley.

PFC Morris Walker, twenty-three, from Fayetteville, North Carolina, killed when an improvised explosive device discharged near his vehicle. Walker was not married but is survived by immediate family including his mother and sister.

ACKNOWLEDGMENTS

I would like to thank Lisa Jensen for the continued assistance in this project.

Without you, this would not be possible.

I would like to thank the Bravo Badgers—Justin, Joe, Tommy, Mark, Eric, and Rico—for their hard work and efforts that allowed me the time to work on other tasks and for our mission to be a success. It would not have happened without having these guys on my side. Just remember, the vanilla gorilla loves you.

I would like to say thank you to my lovely wife and great children. You are the *best*!

Thanks to the best skipper a sailor could ask for and a master chief that cares for her sailors like her own children. A thank-you isn't enough!

I would also like to give praise to God for allowing me this opportunity and placing all the above people in my life. God is good (Psalm 73:28)!

INTRODUCTION

I grew up in rural America, raised to work hard and be proud of my country. Every generation of my family served in the military, and living in an atmosphere like that, I felt an overwhelming sense of pride in America. During that time, patriotism was common where I lived. We pledged allegiance to the flag before school assemblies, stood for the national anthem at football games, and got an inspirational boost every time we heard songs like Lee Greenwood's "Proud to Be an American" or "America the Beautiful" performed by anyone, from Ray Charles to Elvis.

When 9/11 happened, it hit me hard, as it did most Americans. We didn't have to live in New York or have friends or family die in the tragedy to take it personally. Many of the people I talked to were angry that anyone, any group, would be bold enough to declare war on the United States by attacking civilians. I watched friends and family in the military deploy, and older friends who had retired returned to their special ranks in the Navy. Wanting to do my part, I joined the Navy, hoping to get to punch a terrorist in the face if not at least find an answer to the question everyone was asking: "Why?"

As the Afghan war progressed from 2001 forward, I watched and waited, along with most red-blooded Americans, for the gloves to come off. We had been attacked by terrorists on our own soil. We didn't need to win hearts and minds. We needed to fight the war like we wanted to win it, give those terrorists a good old-fashioned ass kicking. We needed to choke out the opponent so that the next time someone said "Hey, here's a suggestion. Let's attack America," the enemy leader would remind his subordinate how bad the ass whooping was last time and beat the holy hell out of him for even thinking something like that out loud.

But the war only dragged on through the double terms of two presidents, and terrorism remained alive and well. Our military's plans were constantly televised, giving the enemy more than fair warning that we'd be coming "on the third Wednesday of next month" or some other absurdly specific date. When I heard the news that the Taliban had an American POW, my heart sank. One of our guys had been captured, and God only knew what he was going through. Was he being tortured? Would he make it out alive? At the time, I didn't pay a lot of attention to how he had been caught. All I cared about was that he was a US soldier, and I kept an eye and an ear out for any news I could get about him. I wondered what was happening to him and tried to imagine what he was going through. I would catch small glimpses of him from now and then when the news would show footage of videos the Taliban were making, watching him get thinner and thinner over time. My civilian job is as a detective for the local sheriff's office, so it was natural for me to mine each video for clues about where he was being held, wondering if the terrain in the background was Afghanistan where he'd been captured, or if there was subtle evidence that he'd been taken out of the country. As scraps of information came to light, I started to notice unlikely synchronicities and odd coincidences.

For one thing, Sgt. Bowe Bergdahl and I are both from Idaho, and I found it weird that we traveled to the other side of the world before our lives intersected. When I learned that Sergeant Bergdahl was from my home state, it brought the war and its baggage closer to home. Eventually, I found out that the name of his task force shared the same name with the town I lived in: Blackfoot. And then there was my assignment in Afghanistan. I ended up serving in a military detention facility, working directly with prisoners who knew where he was and what it would take to get him released. Although I've used the term *coincidence*, it's only for the lack of a better word. Hindsight is 20/20, and looking back over the events, the part I played in Bowe Bergdahl's release—though a small part—couldn't be coincidence. It was fate. God always has a plan, and I got drawn into that plan in a way I could never have intended or imagined.[i]

It wasn't until Sergeant Bergdahl had been released that I finally started to learn more about the circumstances of his capture. I heard the same stories everyone else did—that he had "wandered off" from his base, that he was a deserter, that his own unit wanted him shot for treason. During my time at the detention facility known as Sabalu Harrison, as the story unfolded, I was consumed with the thought of helping bring home the only POW from the United States. Many others had been working for years to find Bowe and bring him home, and I wanted to help however I could. Visualizing the US Army taking custody of him from the Taliban, the sense of purpose and pride was tremendous. However, as the questions began, as rumors of a trial were circulated, as outcries for court martial sounded from every corner of the country, the honor I felt over playing a part in the release turned to shame. I started to second-guess myself and wonder what I had done. Did I do the right thing? On one hand, of course, bringing him home was the right thing. The United States never leaves anyone behind, so I tried to hold onto that as confirmation that what we had accomplished was honorable and that we'd done right by an American soldier. On the other hand, learning he'd willfully walked away from his post left me torn inside.

Possibly, telling this story will help me come to terms with the good and bad feelings I still harbor. Everyone is familiar with the capture and release of Bowe Bergdahl, but the only details they know about how either came about is what they've heard in the media. I cannot shed any light on the truth of his capture, but I can share my experience at Sabalu Harrison, and that is what I've chosen to do in writing this book. The experiences at the detention facility I describe are accurate, although some details and names have had to be omitted or changed out of necessity and because of security. The title of this book, *24/1*, refers to the actual numbers the Taliban originally were trying to negotiate in exchange for Sergeant Bergdahl's release: twenty-four of their guys for one of ours. The part of the story that pertains to Sergeant Bergdahl's experience was written based on a transcript of a statement (available online) that he gave to the US

Army at the Joint Base in San Antonio, Texas, in addition to media interviews and reports. Many names, battalion numbers, and other identifying designations have been changed to protect others as well as myself.

Thousands have lost their lives in this war, but six lives may have been spared if not for the turn destiny took when Sergeant Bergdahl chose to go outside the wire that fateful day in July 2009. His unit had been scheduled to leave the area but stayed on longer than planned to search for him. Many of the subsequent missions after he disappeared carried a secondary priority of keeping an eye out for him or finding him. What's more, the search for the sergeant resulted in tension and ill will from locals. Although the official word is that no men lost their lives trying to find and free Bowe Bergdahl, that word is based on a technicality. Six men did lose their lives, whether you consider it a direct or indirect result of Sergeant Bergdahl going outside the wire, and that's why this book is dedicated to them and their families—to honor them and make the statement that they will never be forgotten.

PROLOGUE

DUSTWUN

July 9, 2009

Taliban—these guys had to be Taliban. Simple villagers wouldn't be carrying AK-47s. Besides, why else had they blindfolded him, tied his hands behind his back, and drove away with him on the back of a motorcycle? He knew he was in over his head. The minute he realized they'd spotted him—when he'd been walking in broad daylight instead of at night because he wanted to make up lost time—he knew he wasn't dealing with local villagers. He also knew that they knew they'd found something valuable.

He realized there wasn't anything he could do, at least at the moment. He shifted into survival mode and tried to work the blindfold up enough to create a gap so he could see where they were taking him. "They" were about six guys, and none of them spoke English. When they first found him, they went through his pockets and took the few things he'd brought with him: his wallet and dog tags, his compass and knife. Now, wherever he was being taken, he was definitely on a detour from his original plan.

It had been a fantastic idea. He didn't regret it, not just yet, but he did regret getting caught. Of course, it had always been a possibility, but it was one he thought he'd made allowances for to ensure it wouldn't happen. That's why he had been traveling at night. Well, at first. If it hadn't been too dark to see his compass, he might almost be at the Sharana base by now. It was what, ten, maybe twenty miles from the outpost where he'd been stationed? It should have been a cakewalk, straight across a flat landscape. He'd run the simulations in his mind as he pulled guard duty, endless hours that would have otherwise been mind-numbing and boring if he hadn't had a plan to map out.

He'd known for a while that he had to do something. This "army" he was in was nothing like he'd imagined. Instead of being a unit of reliable, highly-trained soldiers anyone would be proud to serve with, he was assigned to a team of guys who were in it just for the paycheck and would grab any chance they had to slack off. Instead of serving a tour to help make the world a safer place to live in, easy money and spare time to perfect their video game skills were all these guys were interested in.

And who could he go to? The so-called leaders were every bit as bad. The ones who weren't on an ego trip, drunk with the perceived power of being a commanding officer, were either busy looking for ways to do as little as possible or, at most, would have simply told him, "That's the way it is. You're a private. It's not your job to say what's right or wrong. Just keep your head down and do what you're told."

There was supposedly an open-door policy in the military these days, but he didn't think going straight to a general or a colonel would do any good. Sure, they would be required to invite him into their offices and politely listen to what he had to say. They might even promise to "look into it." In the end, though, he was sure they would disregard his complaint as the grievances of a disgruntled or disillusioned person.

No, his plan was the only thing that would get him taken seriously by the right people. He'd seen "DUSTWUN" written somewhere and asked one of the guys in his platoon what it was. His buddy told him that when a soldier is taken or disappears, a radio signal goes out: *DU*ty *ST*atus *W*hereabouts *UN*known. DUSTWUN— from that one word, everyone knows that someone is missing, but it's not only the immediate unit that knows something is going on. The call goes all the way up the Army chain of command. It goes to the Marines. It goes to the Air Force. If he disappeared from the Mest

Outpost, a DUSTWUN would be called, and everyone would be aware of it. But then, what if he reappeared in a safe place, like the FOB at Sharana? It might take him a full twenty-four hours, maybe as long as two days to get there, but then the right people would not only have to listen to him, but they would also *want* to listen. They'd want to know what the hell happened, and he'd be in the position he needed to be to reveal what so badly needed to be exposed. When he would be escorted in to see the general, the officer would take him seriously when he would announce that the base commander, the sergeant major, and a host of others were unfit to serve in those positions, that they were creating a dangerous environment for the men under their command. He could then demand that an investigation be launched and psychological evaluations be administered. Once that was done, the only logical conclusion would be the removal of the unfit from duty.

The motorcycle carrying him hit a bump, and he was jarred back to the present, a reality that didn't match his plan. It was a last-minute decision to revise the plan that led him off track and into the hands of the enemy. About twenty minutes after going outside the wire at Mest, he'd panicked a little. Being away from the outpost in the complete blackness of the Afghan night, he'd realized the true seriousness of what he was doing. When he got to Sharana, they would charge him with everything they could. However, if he were to arrive with something valuable, an additional reason for leaving the command post other than getting an audience with a general, it might take the edge off the trouble he was in. What if he could bring along some valuable intel with him to Sharana?

Improvised explosion devices were an issue in the area. The Taliban had been planting IEDs along roadways, in culverts, and trenches and were blowing up military vehicles on a regular basis. What if, while he was on his way to Sharana, he came across people planting IEDs? He could follow them back to their camp or wherever they came from and could then use the information as leverage that might minimize the trouble he was in. Sure, he'd gone outside the wire, but they would have to weigh that against him returning of his own free volition and bringing along intel that could result in tracking down the people who were jeopardizing American lives.

He knew he could handle a mission like that. He'd been wanting to go into Special Forces for a while, and this was exactly the type of thing he imagined SF did, no special training, no science-fiction technology. They relied on their own physical capabilities and their common sense. They were sent out to do a job, and they got it done, just like he would. He'd grown up in the mountains of Idaho, terrain that was strikingly similar to where he was now. Long before he'd joined the Army, he'd conditioned himself to run long distances in the climate and high altitude of the Idaho wilderness. It would be all in a day's work for him, and soon he would be back at the FOB, having earned an audience with someone in power, and he would bring along bonus information that might even get him to the qualification course for Special Forces. The icing on the cake when he made this mission a success is that it would allow him to prove to himself and everyone else that he wasn't a failure. That was a label that had defined him ever since his early discharge from the Coast Guard a few years earlier, and one he would be happy to get away from.

As the motorcycle slowed to a stop in front of a ramshackle house, his thoughts of Special Forces faded. He tilted his head back and tried to see as much as he could, which wasn't a lot, before he was pulled from the bike and shoved toward the house. Inside, some of the men went through his things again, while two others used a strap and a piece of rope to reinforce the ties that held his hands in place behind his back. He hadn't given up on escaping yet, but he knew he had to wait for the right moment. He figured that if he didn't resist, his captors would relax and grow careless, and that would be the time to make his move.

He couldn't understand what the men were saying, but it seemed to him that they were trying to locate someone, maybe get orders on where he was to be taken. They put him on the back of the motorcycle again and resumed driving. At one point, they stopped in a village and took pictures of themselves with him as their trophy while the children threw rocks at him, and the villagers had a good laugh. Back on the bikes, they finally found someone on their short-wave radios who spoke English. From the tones of their voices, it must have been who they'd been looking for all along, someone to communicate with him.

They immediately drove to a meeting place in the middle of nowhere, among the ruins of a farm or small village. It turned out that the man didn't speak English very well. Haltingly and with a thick accent he asked, "How are you?" The reply was "Fine," but that was the extent of the conversation. At least the man was educated enough to see that the restraints were cutting off the circulation in his hands. He had the captors take off the straps, and they replaced them with a chain and padlocks. Then they gave the man his wallet and dog tags, and because he knew a little English, he was able to read his driver's license and ID and give them his name.

Then they were off again, motoring to another village where the Taliban guys were well-known. *Maybe it's their hometown*, he mused, noticing that everyone came out to greet them, and the elders seemed particularly pleased and proud of them. They led him to what looked like a meeting hall, then shoved him down on his knees and threw a blanket over his head. He heard their footsteps retreating into the building, leaving him alone with the village children who started throwing small stones and other things at him.

He would have preferred to be alone, but at least this was the chance he'd been waiting for. If he could at least get his hands in front of him and remove the blindfold, he was sure he could outrun the Afghanis. He knew exercise wasn't a priority for them, so he was sure he could evade them if he ran to terrain their motorcycles couldn't traverse. Yeah, there was the chance they might shoot him, but he needed to do something because the situation was only getting worse.

He sat back, trying to get into a position that would allow him to slip his hands under his feet. It was difficult struggling under the blanket, and he gave up on that idea after a few minutes. During the attempt, however, he realized that he could work the blindfold up above his eyes with his knee. Able to see where he was going, he shrugged the blanket off and ran for it. Unfortunately, it wasn't only the children who had been watching him but the rest of the village, everyone who wasn't inside the meeting house with his captors.

They all pursued him, recapturing him only fifty feet from where he'd started.

After that, he was back on the motorcycle and off to another location where they showed him off to a village elder, an older man with a gray beard. First, he was taken inside a house to be presented to the old man, then he was moved to a tent for a while where he was on display like an animal in a zoo. At one point he thought someone might be taking pictures or recording a video of him on a cell phone. Later, he was taken out of the tent and transferred to another house. All that moving around and everything that had happened made it hard to believe it was only earlier that day that this bad dream had begun. Finally, as the sun started going down, they brought him outside and put him in the back of a truck. Someone came up to the side of the vehicle and with a heavy accent asked, "Who are you?" They had his ID. They knew who he was, so he wasn't sure why he was being asked about his identity. Before he could answer though, the man told him if he moved, they would kill him, but not to worry. "We take you to another place."

They were likely looking for the best place to keep him so they could negotiate a high price with the United States for the safe return of an American soldier—at least he hoped a safe return was part of their plan. After all, a dead soldier wasn't worth anything, right? As the sun set on his first day outside the wire, blankets were piled on top of him, and he was driven into the mountains where the group spent the night at a remote house.

As morning dawned, they were up and on the move again, and the next two days were similar—drive all day, stop and spend the night at an isolated house, then back on the road at first light. The third night was different. They drove almost through the night and didn't stop until the sky was turning gray and pink with the first hints of sunrise. When they did stop, it wasn't at a house where they would rest. Instead, his captors led him up a mountain where they presented him to a man they referred to as Mullah Sangeen Zadran. Only later would he fully understand the importance and power of this man who, it turned out, was a commander in the Haqqani Network, an insurgent group of Islamists with close ties to the Taliban. At this point, all he knew was that the man was important enough to command the respect of the men who had been moving him around the country. At least the only orders given that night were to have him locked inside a room, his hands still bound.

CHAPTER 1

June 2012

I'd known for weeks that the orders would be coming, but having them in writing, holding them right there in my hand, suddenly made it all a reality. I was being deployed to the Middle East. It wasn't my first time. As a master-at-arms first class in the Navy, I'd served in Jordan and Kuwait in 2008 and 2009—two places during one mobilization—but because of my patriotism and desire to serve, I had put my name back in the hat for drawing orders immediately after returning home, and it had been there for almost three years. I tried to be patient, knowing that the time would come, and it finally did. Another MA1 by the name of Scott had gotten orders to deploy, but he was nervous about going alone. He'd mentioned his reservations to my master chief, who asked me if I would be willing to mobilize and go along with MA1 Scott. I didn't even have to think about it. My immediate response: "Yes, Master Chief!"

Of course, that was *my* immediate response. My family, my wife, Jean, in particular, wasn't as excited about the orders as I was. There's a real reason people say that the whole family serves, and it's not just patronizing lip service. We go and serve our country, but our spouses get left with all the day-to-day stuff: looking after the house, the yard, the car, taking care of the kids. Families are on a different kind of front lines, dealing with the emotion and the news and all of it. To say it's stressful is an understatement.

Jean had been through it before, so she knew what was coming, but this time, she would be doing it all with three kids as part of the deal. Our daughter is the oldest—almost nine at the time—so she could help out a little with her younger brothers, who were six and one and a half. It was little consolation and not anywhere close to the same as me being there, and Jean was better than me at seeing the whole picture. While my patriotic duty was what I focused on, she was looking ahead at a year or more of being a single parent. On top of that, she had gone back to school and was studying for final exams when I hit her with the news that I had finally gotten the orders I'd been waiting so long for.

"I know this is important, but it's not a good time," she said when I first told her about deploying. "I can't even think about this now. Can we talk about it after finals?"

When we came back to the subject a couple of weeks later, after Jean had passed her tests and didn't have to think about school for a while, the idea still didn't sit well.

"It would be tough to see you go over there and not know what was going to happen to you, even if it was just me to consider. But we have a family now. The first time was hard enough with two kids. Now we have a baby. You're going to miss out on a lot with him— with the other kids too," she argued, tearing up as her voice broke. "We'll miss you. We need you here."

When I had told my master chief I'd be willing to deploy, I didn't immediately think about how hard it would be on my wife and kids for me to be gone, how sad they would be to see me go. I'd miss them too—a lot. My family is everything, but I was looking at it like it was only a year or so out of our lives, a year that could make a difference for everyone, including us.

"Look, it's going to be hard for me too," I told her. "But you know I need to do this. I can do something good over there. There's a war going on, and my training and background can be useful. Besides, with three kids now, we could really use the extra money, and you know how good the military insurance is."

She couldn't deny those facts. It was important to us for Jean to be at home with the kids instead of having to work, but my small-town detective's salary barely made that possible. Serving in the Navy had supplemented my income and provided medical benefits our family needed, the price for making sure they were taken care of. We'd never been the type of couple that fights over anything, but working out the issue over another deployment was as close as we ever came. It still took several weeks of talking and high emotions before Jean came to terms with another tour of duty for both of us. In the end, she found a way to be okay with me going because there was no way she could not. She could see my need to serve practically seeping through my pores. Jean knew I'd told my master chief I was willing and able to deploy, and she could see that, in my mind, I was already preparing to go.

When I had first received the orders through email and printed them off, I eagerly scanned the particulars to find out where I would be going and what I would be doing. I saw that I was being sent to Afghanistan, but when I read the job title, the patriotic soundtrack playing in my head screeched to a halt. The word I saw was "Librarian." The Navy was sending me to Afghanistan to be a *librarian*? My excitement drained away, replaced by disappointment as I thought, "Librarians don't get to punch Taliban fighters in the face. What have I done?"

I hadn't been in a library in I didn't remember how long, and I was sure there was no way I could run a card catalog. When I brought it up to my master chief, asking her which of my skills they'd used to match me up with this job and telling her I'd need a crash course in the Dewey Decimal System, she laughed.

"Trust me," she said. "You are perfect for the job. It's a bad-ass gig, and you won't be disappointed."

That was reassuring, and I did trust her, so I began looking ahead at what would happen before I actually deployed to Afghanistan.

First, I'd have to do a few weeks of training in Texas with the rest of my unit. Essentially, it would be basic military training, a refresher to make sure we were all ready to go into the environment we were being sent to and that we had some basic necessary skills. We had to qualify with weapons, take a combat medical course, and learn how to drive the military vehicles and equipment we'd be expected to operate. As an enlisted man in the Navy, I'd been through a lot of it before to various degrees, but not everyone in the reserves is combat trained. Some could be convenience store clerks in real life or even actual librarians. The group I went with included some military and law enforcement people, but there was also a sculptor, a school janitor, and a few were unemployed. The training in Texas made sure we all had similar skills, if not at the same level, so at least we all knew what was expected of us.

The Navy Reserve Center in Idaho is located in Boise, the state capital. My orders specified that I was to report there on 10 September 2012 to make sure all the paperwork was done. My family drove over with me and accompanied me to the airport afterward for the sendoff. Ham, the lieutenant commander that was the Navy Reserve Center skipper at the time, personally came down to speak to our families and us. He was great, giving his personal cell number with the instruction for our families to call anytime as had my master chief. Jean was still feeling conflicted about me going, so that was wonderful and honestly helped put her at ease to have two people available who could provide information and help 24-7. The VFW and the American Legion were there too, and the public had been invited, so a huge crowd of supporters was on hand to bid us farewell. It was a very proud moment, though I admit it was painful watching my wife and kids standing there, being so strong, supportive, and brave.

When we touched down in Fort Bliss, Texas, we followed the straightforward instructions we'd all been given:

1. Get off the plane.
2. Get your luggage.
3. Stand by the door.
4. Wait for your ride to the base.

There were fourteen of us in all, twelve first-round picks and two alternates who were along for the ride in case someone "washed out." If there were physical issues or something in the background check didn't pan out, that individual would be sent home, and an alternate would take his place.

When we arrived on base, we were directed into a room where long tables had been arranged in a *U* shape. We dropped our gear and introduced ourselves to each other, though many of the guys appeared to have already made friends on the trip over. There was a chief standing in the middle of the tables overseeing the initial meet and greet, and he instructed MA1 Scott and me to pick "teams" so we could break off into two groups for training. He told us that our assignment was Detainee Ops. We would be deploying to Bagram Air Base which was about twenty-five miles northeast of Afghanistan's capital. We would be working at the Parwan Detention Facility, which was effectively a prison located at Bagram. The prison is called Sabalu Harrison, and the inmates are called "detainees," but they are effectively prisoners of war. The detainees being held at Sabalu Harrison had been caught participating in Taliban activities or suspected of having connections to the Taliban. When someone was brought in, a thorough investigation would be conducted to either prove basis for the charges or find the detainee innocent. Naturally, if someone isn't guilty, they are released, but this particular detention facility was the only one in Afghanistan with any level of threat to it. That was because it housed a large population that had indisputable ties to the Taliban, and a handful were men who would be there for pretty much the rest of their lives because of the danger they posed if they were set free.

Once we knew the basics about where we would be going, the chief informed us that the plan was to deploy to Afghanistan after the first of the year.

"If you work hard and training is successful, we can all go home for the holidays before shipping out," he told us. "On the other hand, if you aren't ready, we can't keep that timetable, and we'll have to stay on in Fort Bliss through Christmas and New Year's to go through all the training again and be ready to go on January two."

Of course, we all worked hard and, thankfully, got it done.

Back in Idaho the week before Christmas, I was anxious to see my family. I arrived home to find that those few weeks in training had been a sort of training for them as well. It gave them a taste of what the next year or more would be like. However, like my training, it was more of a simulation than reality. In reality, I wouldn't be in Texas; I'd be in an entirely different country, in dangerous territory, and there would be no coming home for the holidays. It was obvious that Jean and the older kids were more than a little worried and apprehensive. While I was gone, my wife had been struggling with being upset that I was leaving for a substantial amount of time and trying to be okay and deal with everything happening so fast. I felt for her and for the kids, but I knew that more time wasn't the answer. I could have waited and put in for orders years later, and it still would have been hard on all of us for me to leave—maybe even harder in some ways. To help try to ease what we were all going through, we decided to have a low-key holiday and focus it all on our family.

Winter in Idaho is snowy and white, the perfect setting for a traditional Christmas. We did all the typical seasonal things like decorating the tree, Christmas shopping, and driving around to see the decorations and lights. We have family in town, but we pretty much laid low that year, not stressing out trying to make it a perfect Christmas. We tried to concentrate on taking time to be together and absorb each other's company and the holiday spirit. During those couple of weeks, we didn't look ahead or worry about what would come next, and it's actually a pretty good way to approach the holiday season. For the most part, it was an easy time, with just a few tense moments peppered in, but it was exactly what I needed, considering what I was heading for.

I have to admit that New Year's Eve was bittersweet. There were some tense moments as I struggled with preparing myself, doing things like starting to phase out civilian issues and trying to start separating myself from Jean, both difficult tasks considering that I was still at home, surrounded by my family.

Under other circumstances, we would have celebrated with friends or extended family (if I'm not scheduled to work), looking ahead with high hopes for the fresh, new year coming up. New Year's Eve 2012, we still had hope that the year would be a good one, but those hopes were shadowed by the uncertainty of what might happen while I was away. My family needed to believe that everything would be okay, so when I told them that it would be, I did it with all the conviction I could muster. The truth is, although it was intense not knowing what to expect, I did feel an inner peace with deploying again. I knew God was telling me it was going to be okay, so I was honestly able to tell Jean and the kids that everything would be all right, and I hoped they would find peace in my calmness and understand the importance of the mission I was about to serve.

January 1, there was no time to mull over what would happen because everything was underway. I was excited to finally be deploying again, to be active and doing something for the war effort instead of sitting home on the sidelines. However, I couldn't avoid the effect my leaving was having on the family. When Jean made the trip with me once more to Boise so I could fly back to Fort Bliss, I tried to keep the mood and the discussion upbeat on the way. To her credit, she tried her hardest to make me feel like she and the kids would be okay, but I could see she was trying to pull away a little, trying to step back from the situation as a protection mechanism. It was painful to see her go through that, but it was one of the best examples of the kind of person she was and why I love her.[ii]

Back in Bliss, our unit would be heading out the next day, so it was literally grab-your-gear-and-go, but it would still be a few days before we arrived in Afghanistan. We would be flying to Germany first and maybe stopping in Ireland before hitting our final destination. At each stopover, naturally, we couldn't go far because we had to be ready to board and go when the next flight was ready. That meant a lot of downtime but not a lot of time to sightsee or do anything else on the way over, just airport shopping and loads of snacking. With not much else to do, everyone in our unit passed the time talking a lot, sharing concerns, and occasionally, drinking a beer and smoking a cigar while we waited for flights. Some of us had been stationed in the Middle East before, and for others, it was the first time deploying anywhere. Whether they'd mobilized before or not, talking with the other guys provided a chance to get to know each other better and see where they'd fit in different situations, like who you could count on and who you couldn't. None of us knew what situations we would face though. All we could hope for was to make a positive impact and serve our country well.

CHAPTER 2

When you think about flying into Afghanistan or any place considered a war zone, the scene plays like a classic war movie. You picture the place landing under fire, the chaos of people running for cover, the harsh environment, and you envision being shot at. You think you're going to have to hit the ground running for cover, dodging bullets. The reality wasn't that exciting. As we approached the landing field, I was struck by how much the terrain resembled my home state. The Southeastern corner of Idaho is considered high desert. The mountain ranges and the climate are a lot like they are in Afghanistan. The base we had been assigned to was located on a plain, dry and spotted with the few plants that thrive in that arid environment. I recognized the sagebrush from back home, but the area was devoid of the evergreens, poplar, and oak trees that grow in the mountains of both Afghanistan and Idaho. The familiar surroundings were comforting to a degree. I wouldn't say I felt at home, but having recognizable landmarks helped alleviate my anxiety about what lay ahead.

Once we landed in Afghanistan, our trip still wasn't quite over. The airstrip we landed at was a few miles from Bagram Air Base, so we had to take a bus to get there. Some of the roads were paved, but it was still a trek through the desert and not exactly a tour sightseers would choose to take. As the base came into view, the reality of actually being in Afghanistan started to hit. This was it. This was where I'd be working and living for about the next twelve months. Having already served a tour of duty, that was the aspect I could relate to, the one that finally made it real.

Once the unit arrived at the facility, we started unloading gear and tried to get our bearings. There were a few pieces of business that couldn't wait, so after everyone was accounted for, we got our IDs and our job assignments. Fortunately, even though everyone knew what they would be doing, we weren't expected to jump right in and get to work. A couple of days had been set aside for us to acclimate, get over the jet lag, and get settled.

Overall, the first day in Afghanistan was pretty easy. We were shown where we would be living, and everyone called home to let family and friends know that we made it. It had only been a few days, but I already felt like a stranger during my call home, like I was calling from an entirely different world. It was weird to be standing in Afghanistan asking about the kids and hear Jean recount the same silly things the kids usually did.

When I asked "How are you doing so far?" she said "Fine," but I could hear the worry in her voice even though I knew she was trying to hold it back.

It was the same for me. I couldn't be honest and tell her the things that were really going through my mind. It would only have added to her worry. On top of that, making small talk beyond asking "How are you?" was almost impossible. Our instructions for Operational Security (OPSEC) prohibited talking about anything specific like the surroundings or the weather. We couldn't risk intel getting out about the base or our families, so avoiding details was for everyone's protection, including the people back home.

After we unloaded and unpacked in our living quarters, we were taken on a tour of the base. It was huge, kind of like a small city. The base has many of the things you would find in a town, such as offices, a hospital, buildings full of dormitory-like rooms for personnel, and even a Burger King. Additionally, there were a few things that weren't likely to be in many cities including a double runway large enough to accommodate all sizes of military aircraft. We familiarized ourselves with the layout so we would know where to go to report for our various jobs and where important places like the laundry, mess hall, and gym were in relation to our living quarters. We would be staying on the base 24-7. Of course, we'd get to rest and would be given more than reasonable amounts of time to eat, do laundry, and work out too. It wasn't a restrictive atmosphere at all, but we were in the middle of the Afghani desert. It's not like there was anywhere to go or anything interesting to see. We were there to work, and that's what our lives would revolve around for the duration of the time we would be in the country.

Sabalu Harrison, the actual prison part of the Parwan Detention Facility, was made up of over a dozen buildings referred to as houses. Within each "house" was a variety of different-sized cells in which the prisoners were kept. There were typically twelve cells to a house, and some were big enough to hold up to thirty men, while others were smaller and would only accommodate three to four prisoners. The US military took pains to assign cells properly. They took into consideration the detainees' ethnicity in relation to the tribe they were from, the region they were captured in, their religious beliefs, traditions, and customs and tried to house prisoners with similar backgrounds together to avoid violent incidents that could result if men from opposing tribes or beliefs were put in the same cells. Taking those measures kept the aggressive outbursts to under 1 percent, an impressive result considering the level of hostility from the detainees.

Parwan was divided into two sides, "ours" and "theirs," so some of the houses were under US control, and Afghanistan had jurisdiction over the others. Having two different areas for prisoners served two purposes. First, the ultimate goal was to turn the prison over to the Afghanis, so setting them up with a section of the prison entirely their own was supposed to give them a chance to get familiar with running that sort of facility. Second, our side of the detention center housed the prisoners who were considered to be the most dangerous. Everyone who was brought in was kept in segregation on the US side until it was determined that their ties to the Taliban were nonexistent or insignificant at most. Once it was established that they played no crucial part in the war, they would be transferred to cells on the Afghan side of the facility.

Over time, I learned that getting moved out of the US side was like a get-out-of-jail pass. The Afghani general on "their" side would routinely let prisoners go free if they could pay. The rumor was that he was taking ten thousand dollars to thirty thousand dollars per person to let them out. Often, someone who was transferred one evening would be gone from the base by the next morning. Sometimes seventy-five to one hundred prisoners would disappear and, if asked where they'd gone, the Afghan military response was "We don't know." What actually would happen was that detainees were simply released right out the front gate to family members and would return to whatever they were doing prior to their capture. Those in charge on the US side weren't naive. They knew what was going on, but what could they do about it? We weren't there to micromanage the Afghani military, so all the US could do was accept the lame answer and keep the highest-risk prisoners in custody on our side of the facility. Still, it was unsettling to know that on any given morning, up to one hundred people walked free who had been detained for being involved on some level in the war—and there they were, a few hundred yards outside the fence around the base, close enough to attack if they wanted to.

As the weeks passed, I began to see that my unit had been dumped into a unique and difficult situation. Not only was the entire facility as a whole in transition, the US side specifically was undergoing a sort of change. My unit consisting of twelve men was all Navy, but we'd been assigned to a facility run by the 636th Military Police Brigade, an Army unit. There was a larger Navy unit there that we weren't attached to, and our arrival overlapped with their departure. They were in the process of getting ready to pull out within a couple of months after my unit got to the base.

My unit would be taking over where the other Navy unit left off, so there had to be a certain amount of cooperation, but we didn't report to them. Instead, we reported to the Army, which made for an awkward dynamic because the Army and the Navy don't operate identically. More than once, I was conflicted about which protocol to follow. After all, we had been deployed by the Navy, but we were working under Army command who expected us to know and follow Army rules and regulations. We were twelve Navy guys in with the Army, and we couldn't even count on the other Navy unit if an issue arose. We all had similar thoughts running through our heads.

What do we do? Whose rules were we supposed to follow? What happens if something gets weird?

The back story I was given about the 636th Military Police Brigade was that it used to be the same unit that ran Abu Ghraib. I tried to validate that but wasn't able to. More than one person from the group told me though that the entire unit was actually the infamous one that had been running things when the abuse scandal broke. The incidents were said to have been confined to two cell blocks, but the level of violence and cruelty was deemed torture, and talk of the abuses was kept alive in the media for years. To this day, almost anyone would immediately know what you're referring to if you mention the name Abu Ghraib.

Abu Ghraib was a huge disaster for the military, so the entire brigade—the ones who weren't serving time in military prisons or who hadn't been discharged—had been put on a shelf. But the Army couldn't keep a nearly intact unit in a box indefinitely, especially while a war was going on. The powers that be must have figured the general, command sergeant major, and everyone else who didn't have a role in the abuse could be used at the Parwan Detention Facility. After all, running a detention center was what they knew how to do, even though their specific brigade number was tarnished.

At least I can say from personal experience that whether or not the 636th was the unit in charge of Abu Ghraib, no abuses or violence were committed against detainees at Sabalu Harrison while I was there. The general wanted to avoid any negative publicity, so prisoners were treated very humanely. Inside all the cells, everyone had mattresses to sleep on. There were toilets, and of course, they were fed a diet prepared by Afghan people, food they would eat if they were living at home, maybe better and definitely on a more consistent schedule. To someone like me who works in law enforcement in the United States, it wasn't what I'd call a prison. The Parwan Detention Facility wasn't anything you or I would consider luxury accommodations, but for a lot of those guys, it was. There were prisoners who would tell you, "I get out of here, I'm going to commit a crime and come back." They were sheepherders, very poor people, so I guess you couldn't blame them for wanting a warm place to live where they had friends to talk to, and they'd get to eat regularly.

Then there was segregation located on the US side of the facility. It was for the detainees who, without a doubt, had ties to the Taliban, and typically, they were strong ties. If someone was in segregation, they usually had a high rank and detailed knowledge of the Taliban's activities and the whereabouts of key players in addition to other important information. They were considered dangerous, and most of the people in segregation were likely to spend the rest of their lives there.

Still, the accommodations weren't that bad. The cells in segregation were built to house individuals so rather than sharing a large room with several people, the segregated detainees spent most of their time alone. The cells weren't very large. Basically, there was room for a twin mattress, a sink, and a toilet, and that was it. The detainees were allowed to keep prayer mats and other religious items. Meals were brought to them, delivered through the "bean slots" in the doors, and they were allowed to have books too, including Qurans. Everyone had one, and the Red Cross would come in and bring them other books as well.

The isolation was probably the worst part of being in segregation. The detainees in the general population part of the prison at least had each other to talk to when boredom set in. The walls of the cells went up about twelve feet, and they didn't have ceilings, but they did have metal mesh mounted across them. That made it possible for detainees in segregation to hear each other and talk, but the guards wouldn't let them converse freely. They were resourceful, though, and would pull threads from their blankets or clothing to make lines long enough to cast a message from one cell to the next. Sometimes they would tap on the walls between their cells too, but the guards would usually put a stop to even those attempts at communication. With prisoners in segregation, it wasn't probable that getting to know their neighbors was the motivation for wanting to communicate. No matter how a conversation might start, it would typically lead to some sort of trouble, anything from initiating hunger strikes to planning escape attempts.

Bagram Air Base is one of the largest military bases the US has in Afghanistan, and there are hundreds of detainees housed at the Parwan Detention Facility on the base. It took several days to show us around after our unit arrived. In fact, although I'd been sent to Afghanistan to work as a librarian, I didn't see the library for over a week. When I finally made it there, it was on a tour of the base. It was nothing like what you might envision when thinking about a library. Instead of being a stately brick building furnished with beautifully carved furniture polished to a high sheen and housing infinite rows of books and all manner of reading materials, the one at Bagram was a makeshift structure about sixty-five to seventy-five feet long by twenty to thirty feet wide. Located next to the Counter Insurgency Task Force (COIN) office, the walls of the library and the shelves inside were made of plywood. There was no roof, but it would have been difficult to get in if anyone had the notion to climb the walls. There were catwalks across the top, but they were only there so the guard force could keep an eye on the place. When we were shown where the library was, most of the books had been removed, and it was boarded up with padlocks securing the entrance. There were cameras trained on the doors, and a verbal warning was given to anyone who had access to that part of the building: Do not go near that room. Do not touch that door!

The official explanation was that it had been closed down after the highly publicized Quran burning on the base the year before. The incident was a major black eye for the military, and the news everywhere continued to publicize the incident. It was a story that wouldn't die, so access to books through the library at Sabalu Harrison had been stopped immediately to eliminate the possibility of it happening again. My orders stated that admission was restricted and passes had to be obtained to gain access. In very special circumstances, certain personnel would be allowed in, but they would have to have the proper paperwork on them to get into the library.

The rumor about the Quran burning was that a Navy guy and two or three Army guys were passing out books to detainees who would then write coded messages in them, and the books would get shuffled around. Basically, prisoners were using copies of the

Quran to pass notes to each other, and it was estimated that up to three-quarters of them contained radical and/or terrorist content. Once that was discovered, the books were confiscated and ordered to be destroyed. You don't have to follow the news to know about the uproar that caused. Since the Afghan National Army (ANA) had personnel shadowing all the Army and Navy people in preparation for taking over the Parwan Detention Facility, they participated in collecting the books, but the ANA claims they warned the US military against damaging them. ANA soldiers could have been involved in the burning at some point, but that wasn't a detail that was seriously considered or even looked at. The point was that the US military was seen as intolerant and aggressively offensive to the Muslim religion, and it was going to end somebody's career. When I arrived at the base almost a year after the fact, the burning incident was still under investigation, so the library remained boarded up, and no one from either side was to enter it.

With no library to oversee, I wouldn't be a librarian after all. Actually, that was a relief. Although my master chief had promised me an exciting assignment, I couldn't ever reconcile that to cataloging reference materials and checking books out to detainees. At least being reassigned might mean a job I could get excited about. The truth was that a lot of the guys didn't end up working in jobs they'd originally been assigned when they got their orders. Jobs changed fast, and they changed pretty regularly.

CHAPTER 3

When it became clear I wouldn't be a librarian, the first job I was given was in COIN, the Counter Insurgency Task Force. In fact, many of us were assigned to COIN initially. Our group was Detainee Ops, and we had a two-part assignment. First, we were tasked with collecting information from the men inside the prison. Anything and everything could be useful because all of the detainees were prisoners of war, so any small hint of a riot, plans for a breakout, or acts of violence toward the guard force was to be reported. Doing the first part effectively meant that the second element to keep the atmosphere inside Parwan tolerable for everyone could be accomplished.

After only three or four days, my job changed again. More accurately, I was given an additional assignment. Although I was still considered a part of COIN, a chief warrant officer (CW) with the 636th moved me to Afghan Intelligence. They called it TA2 (Train, Assist, and Advise). It was part of the plan to turn the facility over to the Afghan government so the Afghan military could run it. Once you get to know the Afghani people, you realize that they don't do things like we do. It's a perfect example of differences in cultures, and it was cause for huge concern that they wouldn't be able to handle the facility once we turned it over. To remedy that, the TA2 program was developed. It was a mirroring strategy to try to teach them to do what we do. For instance, if a US prison guard were watching a group of detainees, then there would also be an Afghan prison guard watching the US guard's every move and hopefully learning from him.

That meant most of my days at first were spent with two to three other people: one or two members of the Afghan military and an interpreter. However, since I still had a role with COIN, I would work nights in Detainee Ops. At first, it was easy to keep the two jobs separate—days with TA2, nights with COIN. Later on, both positions would turn into full-time jobs, and the duties sometimes overlapped. That meant I would have to shift gears often in a twenty-four-hour period, going from one job to the other and back again. It kept me busy and moving most of the time, which I didn't mind at all. I felt useful, and the constant work kept my mind off not being at home.

At least both jobs were at the same facility. I might be running from one end of the base to the other, but that was the extent of the commute. Still, it was inconvenient to maneuver at times. In splitting up the detention center and working out a plan to turn everything over to the Afghani people, it was determined that it would be best for each side to have separate access points, so there was an Afghan entrance on their side and a US entrance on our side. The sides were restricted too, so Afghan military personnel couldn't freely come over to our side, and we couldn't just walk in over on their side either. Requests for permission had to be submitted and approved. Anyone visiting one side from the other had to have a memo and usually had to be escorted by someone from the other side. Eventually, those rules relaxed for me, but at first, there was an entire process to go through to make a visit to their side no matter what the reason was.

The differences between the Afghan military and the US became clearer the longer I worked in TA2. Procedures and protocols that might seem common sense to you or me go over their heads and don't even occur to them. How the ANA dealt with contraband taken from prisoners is a perfect example that has stayed with me vividly because of the illogical and absurd way it was handled.

There were a number of things that detainees weren't allowed to have, so we had to train the Afghani guards to search the prisoners and their cells on a regular basis and confiscate anything that might be able to be used as a weapon. The contraband was supposed to be secured in the intel office, but that was where official procedure broke down. I visited the room for the first time within a day or two of starting my job with TA2 and found an entire metal wall covered with Ziploc baggies.

"What's all this?" I asked the Afghani guard I'd been assigned to work with that day.

"Contraband from the cells," he replied.

I looked closer. Every baggie had a number scrawled on it, and each one held one or two contraband items, such as thread and needles, shanks, messages—pretty much anything and everything prisoners would want to hide. All the smuggled or handmade illegal items found in the cells were brought to the intel room as instructed. The Afghani guards would put the contraband in baggies, seal them, use a marker to write the prisoner's number on the bag to indicate who the item was taken from, then use tape or a magnet to hang the bag on the wall.

"You guys don't have a chain of custody?" I asked, my American law enforcement background showing. Forget that the items on the wall weren't in any sort of order by date or prisoner number or even grouped according to how hazardous they might be. Everything was just hanging on the wall of a public room for anyone to grab. US personnel were typically escorted into the room by ANA personnel, so the office was frequented by both the US and Afghan sides, and officers and enlisted people had meetings in there all the time. We were advised that up to 90 percent of the Afghan guards were dirty, so I had to wonder what's to stop a guard from grabbing a shank and taking it back in to give to the prisoner it was taken from or to a different prisoner? Later, I learned that is exactly what happened. Contraband such as razors and shanks never remained on the wall for very long. I was advised that guards would take those items and reintroduce them into the facility. Although the detainees at Parwan were united in their hostility toward America, they were all from different regions of the country, so many also disliked and mistrusted each other and needed protection within their cells.

The ANA guard I was talking to looked at me, uncomprehending. He didn't have a clue what "chain of command" meant. All he knew was that they were supposed to bring contraband to the intel office. Beyond that, he didn't have any idea that what they were doing was dangerously inadequate. He probably thought they'd been doing a great job of dealing with it all. They simply don't have the inclination or organization skills to handle things like that the way we would in the US.

Finding stuff to fix and change was what I did best, so I recruited some of the Afghan guards to help me build some evidence boxes. I located a shipping crate on the Navy side of the facility and had the guards divide it into two boxes. We put a lid with slots cut into it on the top, positioning a slot over each box, and added small doors to the bottom with hinges and padlock hasps. I had the boxes painted red and marked "CONTRABAND." A ledger was attached to the top of each of the boxes by the slots, fastened in place with screws so they couldn't be misplaced, and both boxes were secured with padlocks.

"Here's the new procedure," I explained. "When you confiscate illegal items from the prisoners, record the information on these logs in sequential order. The date, the time, who you took it from, and what it is. Then write the same information on the bag before dropping it in the slot."

I gave the intel guys the keys to the locks so they could come in periodically to take the evidence out of the boxes and dispose of it. A seemingly simple solution but one that no one had thought to implement. I learned that over the years, others had submitted ideas about alternative ways to deal with the contraband, but they were all rejected. My idea was easy for the Afghan National Army to follow so they could track and document all the contraband they collected from the cells. Because the ultimate plan was to turn everything over to the ANA, implementing procedures that they could independently maintain was a priority, and coming up with this protocol resulted in a pat on the back from the US Task Force as well as contributing to Brigadier General Eggers signing off on a citation for me.

Probably the biggest difference between my plan and others that were put forth was that I simply came in and did it without asking for permission or approval. I would end up operating that way a lot while I was at Sabalu Harrison. You have to walk a fine line to do things that way in the military though. Typically, nothing is done without running it through the chain of command and getting authorization from everyone above you. I wasn't putting anyone in danger though, and as long as I was actually improving conditions, nobody seemed to mind that I wasn't going strictly by the book.

I may have had an unconventional way of getting things done, but my tendency to be a problem-solver influenced what job I eventually ended up with. My chief warrant officer saw that I wasn't afraid to take the initiative to get things done, and little by little, he took the leash off to see what would happen.[iii] As long as things kept turning out positive, I had more breathing room to do the jobs I was given as well as some that weren't assigned to me but that I simply took on. It all came together fluidly, and looking back, I have to explain it as *divine* plan. Everything seemed to fall into place too easily for it to be coincidence, chance, fate, or any of the other words people use to try to rationalize the unexplainable. Still, I operated under the real fear of something going wrong. As long as things went well, that was great, but if things didn't continue to fall into place, there was no coverage. I was working without a net.

Right about the time my CW was getting comfortable with letting me do my thing, I was assigned to handle hunger strikes in the prison. They would happen frequently and for various reasons. One, two, or an entire group of prisoners in a house or across multiple houses would suddenly stop eating and drinking. Sometimes they'd demand to be allowed to observe a specific religious holiday, sometimes they'd strike because they wanted a special food, and sometimes it was just a way to assert some control over their situation.

All hunger strikes have key principals in common. They are nonviolent and declare martyrdom for a cause. The objective is to shame the enemy as a form of manipulation, and hunger strikes are tailor-made for that purpose because of the effects they have. The human body needs about one thousand two hundred calories each day to perform basic functions, so even someone who sits or lies in one place literally doing nothing all day still has that basic caloric requirement for their body to perform things like beating the heart to pump blood and breathing in oxygen and exhaling carbon dioxide. Even the brain activity of a coma patient burns a certain number of calories. What's more, simple tasks beyond sitting motionless, such as standing, walking, talking, or turning the pages of a book require additional caloric intake, so when someone stops eating, his body doesn't get the fuel it needs to exist. Organs can be affected, especially when water is refused too, and chronic diarrhea and kidney problems can result in a matter of days. Skin, hair, and nails become brittle over time, and the skin will eventually crack and develop sores. If the hunger strike isn't ended, the unavoidable result is death. Detainees at Gitmo had died because of hunger strikes, making it a hot-button topic. The last thing the US military wanted on top of the negative press from the Quran burning were reports of prisoners at the Parwan Detention Facility becoming sick or dying as a result of a hunger strike.

Whatever the detainees' reasons were, the minute someone went on a hunger strike, news ran right up the chain of command. Everyone, including the general, was aware of it. "Wait and see what happens" had become the official procedure, but we didn't wait long. If the strike had any momentum, we were to dissolve it ASAP. Knowing that I would figure out a way to resolve the issue, the CW would call me in, tell me which house was staging a hunger strike, and say, "Take care of this."

In my own mind, I'd often think, *How am I supposed to do that?* But I knew better than to ask. There were official ways to end a hunger strike that were effective a lot of the time. For instance, the detainees who were refusing food and water would be taken to the medical section of the facility where they would be put on an IV and be encouraged to eat. Hunger strikes at Guantanamo Bay have gotten a lot of press because the procedure there a lot of times is to force-feed the prisoners, so the way we dealt with it at Sabalu Harrison had to be much more humane.

If the established methods didn't work to diffuse a hunger strike though, I was still expected to make it go away, and no one cared what I did to accomplish that. I was cautious with the first hunger strike they sent me in to break up. I was still a little confused about where I stood. I was in the Navy, and I was only an E6 Petty Officer First Class. Everyone could pretty much dump whatever they want to on me. I was given an order, and I had to follow it, so I just went in there and figured it out, falling back on the experience I'd gained in my civilian profession.

As part of my job in law enforcement in the US, I've worked as a hostage negotiator, and the strategies I learned over the years helped me resolve the hunger strikes at the detention facility in Afghanistan very quickly. A lot of those guys had been in prison for a long time. They didn't get any attention from the guards, so to me, it was simply a matter of giving them the attention they craved. My process was talk, ask a question, listen, ask a question, listen, repeat. I'd go into situations where prison guards had been working with detainees on strike for weeks. It would be to the point where the detainees had been taken to medical, and I could get it ended in a day. It was so effortless, dealing with the hunger strikes became a regular assignment for me in addition to the daily things I'd already been assigned. Officially, I was still doing work for both COIN and TA2, but eventually, every day my CW would call me and say, "Hey, we got another hunger strike. Go over to 'this' house" or "Head over to medical."

My experience as a hostage negotiator was invaluable, but I think the way I treated the detainees who were striking also made a huge difference in my success rate. There were a lot of men in Sabalu Harrison, and everyone was assigned a number. Those numbers were how they were identified when US and Afghani personnel referred to them, and they were used in place of names when addressing them. That always seemed demeaning and impersonal to me, so I would never use their numbers when talking to them. Instead, I would say, "Hey, how are you?" or "Nice to see you" as a way to start off rather than "Okay, prisoner zero-four-one-five-two-seven..." That was just too cold. I would still refer to them by their numbers in my written reports and when talking to other military personnel, but my track record proved that my technique plus listening to what they had to say was effective.

Additionally, I chose not to find out anything about the prisoners. Mostly, I didn't have the time to research their backgrounds. However, I also thought having that information would be unfair. I felt it was better to not know about who I was dealing with so I couldn't pass judgment. I figured if I was unbiased, I wouldn't have a preconceived idea of whether I was going to mistreat a person or not. It is a technique I utilize in my civilian job. When people tell me they are always treated badly because of their history, I can honestly say, "I don't know anything about your history."

I could have asked for information on prisoners and gotten it or simply tracked it down myself, but I felt it was to my advantage to never really know who I was dealing with. Not having that information made it much easier to see the prisoners I was trying to manage as humans and treat them with at least a minimum amount of respect.

CHAPTER 4

Although I work in law enforcement in my civilian job and have experience as a negotiator, trying to do similar work in Afghanistan was hardly comparable. Until you have to work in a war zone, it's hard to imagine what it's like. Almost daily there was mortar fire, small-arms fire, and regular explosions going off outside Bagram Air Force Base. Sure there's a point when those noises can melt into the background, but you still hear them subconsciously, and they make you constantly aware that you're trying to live and work right in the middle of danger. That's a level of stress that has to be experienced to understand.

In addition to the chaos going on outside the facility, turmoil and unrest were regularly going on inside the detention part of the base. That added another layer of difficulty to my job with COIN trying to collect information and head off or at least minimize disturbances and keep the peace. From day to day, I wouldn't know what awaited me when I'd walk into any of the detention houses, and some of them had a reputation for being problems. Although I'd always hold out hope for an easy day with no incidents, it was common for me to walk in on a riot in progress with the detainees shouting and throwing feces and threatening the guard force with acts of violence. Of course the US military wanted to curtail those episodes, but it was a hard issue to get a handle on. Only someone who had the respect of the prisoners had any hope of controlling their volatile outbursts, and it seemed that while the detainees had a certain level of wariness where the guard force was concerned, they didn't necessarily respect them, not even the Afghani guard force.

In hindsight, it's clear that two seemingly insignificant routine events played a big part in gaining the credibility and respect for me from both the Afghan and US sides that allowed me to accomplish the things I did. The first was part of a negotiation I did to end a hunger strike. The men involved wanted to observe an upcoming religious holiday. *Sure, why not?* I thought, thinking that allowing the prisoners to have their holiday would be no big deal. Little did I know what it would involve.

Bit by bit, I began to see what I'd committed to. For the holiday to be celebrated properly, each cell in each house would have to have its own mullah and qāri. As a religious holiday, naturally, someone who was educated in the sacred law and theology of Islam must officiate, so we would need to bring in mullahs. Plus, when the Quran is read, it must be done in a precise manner, with actual rules to the recitation that include reading or reciting the passages using a melodic tone in the voice. The qāris are special readers who are trained and must be certified to perform the job, so we got busy making 175 of the prisoners into qāris for the occasion. Everyone going through the certification had to be able to read and understand what they were reading as well as read according to the rules of proper recitation. The religious advisor for the minister of defense came down and had to sign off on everyone who would be reading for a mullah.

It was a huge undertaking, and that was only one part. On top of certifying the qāris and bringing in mullahs, the detainees who would be serving as qāris would have to be moved from their cells to the recreation yard where the ceremony was to be held without being handcuffed. Both of those issues meant a need for heightened security, and we would have to be aware at all times. Then there were the details like the special food traditionally served during the celebration, and tables and chairs would have to be brought in. Plus, everyone had to dress entirely in white, so we needed a supply of plain white robes and caps. However, the US has a policy that restricts the military from handling religious items, so we had to figure out who would buy the clothing and bring it in. In the end, it took two months to make preparations and arrangements so the detainees could have their celebration, but we did it, and that gave me credibility with the Afghan National Army.

The other thing that happened was a result of me taking charge of the way the guard force dealt with contraband confiscated from prisoners. One day, soon after we'd gotten everything down off the walls in the intel room and into the evidence boxes, the Parwan Detention Facility hosted an important visitor. Dr. Ghani is the current president of Afghanistan, but at the time, he was serving as the minister of finance. He had grown up in Afghanistan, although he had been educated abroad and had earned his PhD at Columbia University in the US. As the minister of finance for Afghanistan, Dr. Ghani is credited with implementing revolutionary reforms in the country and the government like computerizing treasury operations and establishing accountability by instituting regular reporting to the cabinet and other stakeholders, including the Afghani people.

Dr. Ghani is known to be a tough and demanding man, even to the point of being disrespectful of anyone he doesn't consider his equal, which was pretty much everyone. No one at Sabalu Harrison liked dealing with him, and when he was anywhere on the base, the orders were not to get caught in his path. We were told, "Just stay away." In fact, anyone who wasn't on duty was advised to go to their room and lock the door.

He traveled with an entourage of Afghan National Army personnel and US Army officers, and because his reputation preceded him, my heart about stopped when Dr. Ghani and his group came into the intel room while I was there. He'd obviously been through the facility before because he looked up at the wall and asked, "What happened to all the stuff that used to be hanging up there?"

"We made contraband boxes for it all," I told him, managing to remain calm even though I was thinking, *This guy's gonna hang me!*

He asked me to show him what I'd done. After I had explained the new procedure, and he'd inspected the locked boxes, he surprised me by offering his hand.

"Great job," he said, giving me a firm handshake. I am probably one of only a few Americans who ever shook his hand, and that gave me even more credibility. To me, those two events were just another part of the job, but I would soon see how valuable that status and credibility was when I needed to get something done.

CHAPTER 5

The frequency of the hunger strikes seemed to increase, or maybe it was just that I was more aware of them since most of them were being assigned to me. A lot of the time, it would be one, two, maybe three people who wanted to make a statement, but sometimes an entire house would get involved. It was hard to know how word got around to different houses. Maybe the guards relayed messages or passed notes for the prisoners, but when news of a hunger strike started spreading, other prisoners would join the "cause."

I'd only been at the Parwan Detention Facility for about three months when I got called in to handle a huge hunger strike. It had started out with only a few guys, but the momentum grew like a wildfire, and soon there were more than one hundred people who wouldn't eat. The only things my CW told me was that it had been orchestrated by someone in segregation, that upwards of one hundred prisoners were involved, and I needed to get rid of it as fast as possible.

"We don't want publicity on this like Guantanamo," my CW said. "A hunger strike this big can bring negative publicity from all sides—the Red Cross, the media, pretty much everyone. We do *not* want that kind of exposure."

"Okay, I'll do the best that I can," I told him.

What else could I do? I had seen hunger strikes grow to fifteen, nineteen, maybe twenty people, but now we had prisoners wall-to-wall refusing to eat.

When I got to segregation, I was directed to three cells next to each other, all in a row. The guy on the left was pretty interesting. He looked like the peddler from Disney's *Aladdin*, and he was the only one of the three who spoke English. I knew what his prison number was, but he told me his first name was Ajmal. The one in the middle was one of the scariest people I've ever dealt with. He had black hair, black eyes, and didn't respond to anything I said directly to him or through his friend Ajmal. He was emotionless the whole time, but he did make it clear that he didn't trust me and didn't want to have anything to do with me. That one I ended up calling Delawar.

The man on the right was a stoic older man with a shaved head and a long gray beard. He became known as Haji, an awkward derivative of his actual name, but it was easier for my English-speaking tongue to say. The way Haji carried himself suggested he was an important man outside of Sabalu Harrison, and he was obviously the leader of this little group of three detainees. Ajmal preferred not to do or say anything without his approval. Whatever the question or request, often Ajmal's answer was "I'll have to see." I quickly learned that meant he had to confer with Haji first.

As usual, an interpreter had been assigned to go with me to segregation to talk to the three detainees, but I soon began talking directly to Ajmal since he spoke English. It was easier and a more direct and comfortable way to communicate. Not having to rely on a military interpreter put the prisoners at ease too. Still, none of them trusted me and seemed to think I was just another in a succession of Americans who wouldn't listen to them and didn't care about them or what they wanted.

Dealing with these guys was an entirely new experience, and not only because I could speak to them directly. With the past hunger strikes I had worked, the prisoners involved just wanted to be heard. All it took to diffuse the other situations was to let them express their demands, make a small concession (usually diet related), and then they would eat. Mostly, they simply wanted attention, and between listening to them and my habit of treating them like people, they got what they wanted. I have to admit I was a little arrogant going in to talk to Ajmal, Haji, and Delawar because it had been so easy to diffuse the other hunger strikes. I thought I would get this one resolved and be off to my next task within the day. I was certain this one would be like the others, centering on complaints such as "I don't like my cellmates," "I don't like the food," "I don't like being watched all the time," "We want more towels…" or books, a different kind of nuts, or any of a million trivial grievances they came up with to get attention.

These three were different though. When I tried to get them to eat by asking if there was a special kind of food I could bring them, Ajmal responded emphatically, "No! We will not eat your food!"

"Will you just drink a Gatorade then or maybe a protein shake?" I cajoled.

"No! No water, no food! We are prepared to go all the way!"

That was the first time I'd heard that one. I asked Ajmal exactly what he meant by "all the way." The answer was simple and clear: "We are prepared to die for this."

Whoa! Die for what? I hadn't even asked them why they were striking because I thought it would be easy to persuade them to eat. When I asked about their demands, I learned that these three had been in segregation for years, and that they wanted to be moved into a house with other prisoners. They wanted to be treated like the others and eat and socialize with them.

"I've talked to you people," Ajmal told me angrily in his broken but understandable English. "I've talked to your colonels, I've talked to your generals, and this is bullshit. Nothing will change. We've been sentenced to be in segregation, and they will never let us out. We are not happy with that. We want to live out our time in a cell together, with others. Your generals know this. We've asked many times, but we have been denied every time, so we're prepared to go all the way."

Well, wasn't that sobering? After a successful run of dissolving hunger strikes, all of a sudden, this seemed complex.

"Well, I'll see what I can do," I told them, being careful not to commit to anything. I knew from training that I had to be cautious about everything I said. If there was even a hint of a commitment in anything I told them, that could have the opposite effect and escalate the hunger strike instead of ending it. Prisoners had been known to use a hunger strike to bully their jailers into committing to unreasonable demands.

"But why don't you drink something?" I quickly added, trying to get some momentum moving in a positive direction. "Have some Gatorade, just as a show of good faith."

Ajmal scoffed at that. He'd already told me that they'd talked to people much higher in the chain of command than me, and no progress had been made. It made me wonder who they were and what they'd done that the US military refused to take them out of segregation and place them in a cell together. Since I had personal rules against looking up prisoners' information, I had to let go of that issue for the moment. In fact, since they wouldn't budge on eating and drinking, I eventually had to call it a day and let it all go for the time being. Detainees went on hunger strikes all the time. This one would simply be more of a challenge for me than the others, and I was always up for a challenge.

At first, I checked on the three prisoners every day, although I didn't actually pay a daily visit to them. I would ask the guards how Haji, Ajmal, and Delawar were doing, and when I did see them, I treated them with as much respect as I had treated any of the other detainees I'd dealt with. I didn't want them to think that they had the upper hand though, so I'd only go in every couple of days to ask them in person how they were doing and to try to talk them into ending the strike. Nothing worked. They would wave me on, indicating I should keep walking. It all kept coming back to their demand to be taken out of segregation. If I had nothing to report on an impending move, they did not want to talk. Initially, I hadn't done anything about getting them moved because I figured that if people higher up than me couldn't or wouldn't do it, what could I do? After a couple of fruitless visits with the prisoners though, I decided to ask if moving them would be possible. As expected, the answer was a definite and unequivocal *no!* "Absolutely not," the CW told me. "That will never happen. Just stay in your lane, Herbert." Translation: mind your own business.

So I went back to segregation to talk to the detainees. I tried to show them by how I was treating them that I had their best interests in mind. A lot of the time I walked a fine line between negotiating and begging, but that was all I could do to try to get them to eat and drink.

"Hey, how are you guys doing?" I'd ask through the bean slots I'd had the guard force prop open before I took a seat on a folding chair in the hallway outside their cells. "You feel like eating something or drinking a protein shake today?"

Some days Ajmal would have more patience with me than others. He would always speak on Haji's behalf, so he might translate something for Haji, asking how I was doing or how my family was or some other trivial conversational nicety that had nothing to do with the hunger strike. To a point, I got the feeling that they liked me visiting them, whether any progress was being made or not. Then there were other times when they'd obviously decided between themselves that enough was enough, and Ajmal would get right to the point.

"Will you be moving us out of segregation soon, or do we have to go all the way?"

"You know that's not something my superiors will readily consider," I would tell him. "Can't you just eat something or take a drink? Any gesture like that would give me leverage to show you're willing to cooperate, and maybe I could see what we can do about getting you moved."

I had no authority to promise them they could get out of segregation, but with every day that passed, I was running out of options. They hadn't eaten anything in several days and had only drunk enough water to barely keep themselves from dying of dehydration. That's why I wouldn't quite promise that I could get them moved and stopped short of admitting I couldn't make it happen. Every visit would pretty much end the same way, however. Ajmal would talk reasonably with me for a few minutes, then become agitated when he saw that the conversation was going the same way it had with everyone else before me. He would remind me that there was only one thing that would bring an end to the hunger strike and that I knew exactly what that was. That was the cue that the day's visit was over.

To make matters worse, these guys were messing with my track record. At the end of each day, I had to report back to my CW, either in person or by email. He was getting more and more disappointed with my lack of headway, and as the hunger strike dragged on, he pulled me aside one day when I came in to make my report.

"This is what's going on. These guys aren't like all the others I've dealt with. They only want one thing, and that happens to be something I can't authorize," I told him. "They say the only way they'll end the strike is if they get moved out of segregation."

My CW shook his head, looking down at the floor before he responded. He didn't acknowledge the issue about moving them. His reply was to reiterate the orders he'd been giving me over and over ever since I'd first been assigned to this particular hunger strike, only this time there was no pretense of common courtesy.

"Get this fucking handled. Do it now," he said. "This guy can't die. We can't have that kind of publicity."

By "this guy," my CW meant Haji, the older of the three prisoners, but he knew they were all in it together. If I could get Haji to eat, the others would follow his lead. On the other hand, if one died, they all would, and three or more hunger strike fatalities would look worse than one. The pressure was on. I decided to make one more attempt to talk with Ajmal. I'd been there only an hour before, but I went back to see if somehow I could do something that I hadn't done before or say something else that would make a difference. When I tried talking to Ajmal again, he shut down. He said, "I told you what we want. We want out. There's nothing more to talk about."

Walking back to my room, I started to seriously wonder, "Who is this guy? Who is Haji, and why is he in segregation?"

The Army wouldn't even consider moving him, but keeping him alive and healthy was a priority. With all those questions unanswered and a direct order to make the situation go away, I'd have to break my own rule. I had the resources to find out who these guys were. I'd never been tempted in the least to look into the backgrounds of other prisoners I had dealt with in the past, but now I couldn't think of anything but learning more about the three detainees who were more serious about their hunger strike than any other prisoners had ever been.

CHAPTER 6

Working two jobs left little time for investigating Haji, Ajmal, and Delawar. It was almost a week before I had a chance to do some digging. I contacted a guy from the intel community I'd met during training, but it was another couple of days before he was able to get back with me. One evening, before I headed over to start my shift with COIN, my intel contact finally emailed to say he had the information I was looking for.

> I can't give you copies of anything, so there are no attachments here, but I'll be on the base tomorrow, if you have some time.

His email contained this information.

> I can meet with you and brief you on the background of the detainees you asked about.

My immediate reply let my contact know I would make the time to meet with him. In less than twenty-four hours, we were holed up in a private office, going over the bits of information he was willing to share with me. He'd brought a thick file folder along with him, but he ended up only showing me a few pages and verbally relaying the majority of the facts from the dossier.

First, he showed me a page that had a mug shot of a younger Haji in the top right corner. His full name was displayed to the left of the picture, across the top of the page, and almost everything I wanted to know was filled in below.

A chart at the top of it all revealed at a glance the basic information about Haji such as his aliases, his father's name, current residences, the tribe and subtribe he belonged to, and the languages he was fluent in. It wasn't surprising to see that Pashto was the only language listed, but I was a little stunned to see that he was only about forty years old. His gray beard and shaved head, along with his contemplative manner and deliberate way of speaking, made him seem much older than he was.

The profile also listed Haji's insurgent affiliations which read like a Who's Who of terrorism: Taliban, Al-Qaeda, Tehrik-e-Taliban Pakistan, and Hezb-E Eslami Gulbuddin. The Haqqani Network topped the list, and when my contact filled in the details, I realized why the US considered it a priority to keep Haji in segregation.

His father had joined the jihad when Haji was still young. He had essentially gone into terrorism like most kids go into the family business. He'd started out transporting food and supplies to the weapons depot his father ran, then joined in the fight when he got old enough. Haji had become a high-ranking officer in the Haqqani Network and then became an official member of the family when he married Jalaluddin's sister. Jalaluddin Haqqani, a well-known anti-Soviet fighter, is the founder of the Network, and he is married to Haji's sister.

Jalaluddin rose through the ranks of the Mujahideen Army in the 1980s. Considering himself a freedom fighter, he felt strongly about battling against Soviet forces that had invaded his homeland of Afghanistan. The *Wikipedia* entry on the Haqqani Network[1] says that Jalaluddin was happy to take advantage of the support offered by powerful opponents such as our own CIA and Pakistan's Inter-Services Intelligence, who were offering to sponsor Soviet resistance. Jalaluddin grew his forces with masses of volunteers that included Osama bin Laden and Abdullah Azzam, and armed them with weapons supplied by the foreign supporters. After training with the

---

[1] "Haqqani network," 25 April 2017, *Wikipedia, the Free Encyclopedia.*

Haqqanis, bin Laden and Azzam went on to establish Al-Qaeda, and the two groups retain their connection today.

Although they weren't affiliated with each other until the Taliban captured Kabul in 1996 and effectively took control of Afghanistan, the Haqqani Network and the Taliban are closely allied. Their ties are a bit tangled. Jalaluddin served as minister of tribal affairs in Afghanistan after the Taliban took power, but the Haqqanis have maintained their own identity in the terrorist mix. In his report for the Institute for the Study of War, Jeffrey A. Dressler categorizes the Haqqani Network as being included under the Taliban's umbrella officially but says that they retain a marked control and command over their own distinct areas of operation.[2]

While the Haqqani Network is a separate entity from the Taliban and Al-Qaeda, the underlying fact is that they're all on the same side, attempting to carry out a joint mission to obstruct Western influence in Afghanistan and drive out Western military and political endeavors from their country permanently. They want Afghanistan to follow only sharia law, and it is there where the Network deviates from its partners. While the Taliban and Al-Qaeda want global jihad—to impose Islamic law on the world—the Haqqani Network is more concerned about Islamic law within Afghanistan rather than on a worldwide level. Kinder, gentler terrorists who would allow the rest of the world to believe and worship as they wish? Maybe, but the fact remains that the Haqqani Network is neck-deep in jihad, fighting right alongside their radical partners. My contact detailed proof of that, summarizing bits of the report for me from the pages that followed.

Apparently, someone else had requested that Haji be moved out of segregation the previous year. The transfer denial he read from included an itemization of the reasons he was incarcerated, and the narrative of the circumstances surrounding his capture was succinct but comprehensive. He had been targeted for capture because of his direct and close involvement with the Haqqani Network, spe-

---

[2] Jeffrey A. Dressler, "The Haqqani Network: From Pakistan to Afghanistan," October 2010, *Institute for the Study of War*.

cifically because he worked immediately under Sirajuddin Haqqani, Jalaluddin's son and second-in-command. An Afghan partner unit, with the help of the Coalition Forces, had directed an assault on a compound in Afghanistan. As the assault force was taking the compound, three men ran from it and had hidden in a shallow ravine. When they were discovered, it was quickly determined that all three were of interest and that they'd found Haji, the one they were looking for. All of the men were armed with multiple weapons. Plus, when the compound was searched, more arms were found, including grenades, a rocket-propelled grenade launcher, and several RPG boosters as well as AK-47s and numerous AK magazines.

The detainee transfer request denial went on to list three pages' worth of reasons Haji was not only valuable to the US but too dangerous to be let out of segregation. For example, he had facilitated multiple suicide bombers over the years throughout Afghanistan. He'd been personally involved in an attack against convoys of Coalition Forces, deploying anti-tank rockets at them as they traveled on desolate roads. Outposts had been attacked as well as several forward-operating bases; suicide bombers had been trained, housed, and mobilized; and IEDs were placed to create chaos and open the door for ambushes and attacks on US forces and our allies. All of it had been verified through multiple sources, and Haji himself didn't have a history of denying anything he'd done. It was unreal to think of sitting across from him, drinking chai, and talking about everyday, normal things while all the time he had dedicated his life to killing Americans and anyone his religion branded an infidel.

Moving on to Ajmal, my contact made me aware of even more information that had me reconsidering helping them. Ajmal was only ten years younger than Haji, but in the small black-and-white picture my contact showed me, he looked closer to his age. He was fluent in Pashto, English, and Farsi, and his affiliations were with Al-Qaida, so his worldview was less tolerant of Westerners than Haji's. My contact scanned the documentation, then briefed me about Ajmal's close association with several ranking principal players, guys who were Al-Qaida leaders and commanders, including some that had been detained at Guantanamo. He had stellar organizational skills and served as a very effective attack planner and supply route manager. Ajmal used several aliases, and his profile listed one other than Ajmal (the one he'd given me) as his real name. He was an expert at finding people to commit terrorist acts, financing it all with money from Al-Qaida.

My contact explained that most of the reports on Ajmal were too sensitive to be included in the information I was being briefed on that day, but despite that, the basic facts he shared with me showed that there was sufficient evidence to detain Ajmal. Right before he'd been captured, it was determined that he had met with unidentified Americans and a Saudi national to set up a bombing. After they had decided it would be too difficult to execute, the plan was changed to a kidnapping, involving a high-ranking US official, but the official's name wasn't revealed to me. Ajmal had been in contact with a Gitmo detainee through a third party, a man who had also paid for Ajmal's services per the detainee's instructions.

When he was captured, Ajmal had been taken without much incident, but his personal property had gone through ETD testing, also known as explosive trace detection. Everything he had on him at the time was wiped down with cotton swabs which would pick up explosives residue, if there was any. The swabs were put through a machine to perform the test, and more than just a trace amount of powerful oxidizers were found. I was advised that there were enough chlorates and perchlorates found on Ajmal's things that the report noted them to be "significantly above detection limits."

My contact gave me a rundown on Ajmal, similar to what I'd learned about Haji, listing the basic information about his family tree and where he was known to live. He also informed me what personal effects he was carrying at the time of his capture, the very ones that were covered in explosives residue: a passport, a couple of CDs and DVDs, a few pictures, and some handwritten notes. There had also been a cell phone, broken into pieces. When he was taken into custody, Ajmal had tried to break the phone and destroy the SIM card, injuring himself in the process. All parts of the phone were retrieved, but my contact changed the subject, so I figured the information our experts had gotten off the phone was in those classified reports he had mentioned.

I was told that Ajmal had been given a polygraph test. The full report was, of course, classified, but I learned that initially, Ajmal had denied having any associations with Al-Qaida, meeting with US enemies, and having anything to do with planning or executing attacks against the US. My contact advised that the answers Ajmal had given to those questions were untrue but that in a later interview, he had admitted to everything he'd denied and more. Plus, he acknowledged that he would continue his activities if released, making his indefinite detainment a necessity.

There was much less information on Delawar, but what there was explained why he was such a silent menacing figure. Delawar's black gaze glared at me from his mug shot as my contact leafed through the last of the pages in the file, deciding what other information he would tell me. Delawar was from a different village than his two friends, but his affiliations were nearly the same as Haji's: Haqqani Network, Al-Qaida, Taliban, and Tehrik-e-Taliban Pakistan. He didn't have as many aliases as Ajmal did, and Pashto was the only language listed on his profile. It crossed my mind that that might be the reason he never spoke during the interviews, but after learning more, I let go of that opinion.

My contact said that Delawar had been captured at the same time Haji was, in the same raid. After Haji and a couple of other people had fled the compound, the building itself was searched. Many more weapons were discovered, along with a few more men. Delawar was one of them, found hiding under some rugs. He had in his possession a rocket-propelled grenade, an AK-47, and ammunition. However, it was more than his presence at the compound and the weapons he was carrying that landed him in permanent segregation. In the course of questioning, it was revealed that Delawar was Haji's number one bodyguard. The two had been inseparable for years, so Delawar had been in on every destructive, evil scheme Haji had carried out. As Haji's constant companion and subordinate, naturally, Delawar would defer to him and refrain from speaking. He recognized his place and stayed in it. That was fine. The burning stares he trained on me when he wasn't ignoring me altogether spoke volumes and were communication enough.

When my contact was finished, I leaned back in my chair and blew out a sigh. This was exactly the kind of information I went out of my way not to know about the prisoners I worked with. Between the three of them, I couldn't begin to tally up all the destruction and death they'd caused. And according to Ajmal, they'd be happy to get right back to work if given the chance. At least I knew why I hit a dead end every time I brought up moving them out of segregation. Without a move to dangle in front of the prisoners though, I didn't know how I would be able to make the hunger strike go away.

CHAPTER 7

Knowing the backgrounds of Ajmal, Haji, and Delawar helped explain why there was no support on the US side to move them out of segregation. These guys were connected, and it was very likely that rehousing them on the Afghan side of the facility would result in all three walking out one night. The US wanted a resolution, but not if it meant prisoners they considered a threat would go free and return to their previous terrorist activities as we thought they would.

With that understanding came the realization that my hands were tied, more so with these three than with anyone else who I'd ever worked with on a hunger strike. They only wanted one thing, and it was one of the few things that I couldn't make happen. I'd never had to beg anyone to end their strike because there had always been something I could do, whether it was listening to what a prisoner had to say or even bringing him a combo meal from the Burger King on the base. At that point, begging was pretty much all I had left. Having been able to effortlessly diffuse other strikes and not taking any pleasure in the thought of showing weakness, I wasn't looking forward to the next few days. Things were reaching a critical stage though. The three detainees' health was on the brink of faltering, and my superiors expected me to resolve the issue before things got worse.

During our next meetings, I took a more subtle approach. We spent most of our time together talking about practically everything except their demand and the fact that they weren't eating. I would put that issue off as long as possible during each meeting.

"How you guys doing today?" I'd start out, then shift to talking about the weather, their families, all the small-talk subjects that any four guys from anywhere might talk about. During one meandering conversation, I learned that they had been doing their homework on me and had somehow found out a little bit about my background when Ajmal asked, "Do your kids like the snow in Twin Falls?"

He hadn't gotten the town quite right. Twin Falls is about 130 miles southwest of where I lived in Blackfoot, but it was disturbing that he knew I had kids, knew the state I lived in and the approximate area I was from, and knew what the climate was like. He was obviously trying to make me aware of their ability to get information on anyone, including me. Of course it bothered me, but I couldn't let on that they'd struck a nerve, so I kind of laughed and said, "Oh yeah, my kids like snow, but I don't know what Twin Falls is."

Later, when I talked to my CW about it, he just shrugged.

"Well, soldiers talk, and detainees listen. It's all they have to do. We don't know if they overheard some of the new prison guards talking about you and mentioning that you are from Idaho or if maybe they heard it from guys getting ready to leave. They keep their ears open, and soldiers sometimes get lackadaisical with OpSec when they're getting ready to go. Plus, the detainees listen, but they're not afraid to ask, and you know where the ANA guards' loyalties are."

It was true. I'd seen the three detainees ordering the Afghan guards around like they were servants. It wasn't long before Ajmal would snap his fingers and tell the ANA guard to bring me a chair and get me some tea whenever I'd walk into segregation. It was odd, but before I was in front of the cells, I'd have hot tea with sugar and a chair to sit on, not at my request but courtesy of the prisoners' commands.

During those intense days when the detainees were intent on going "all the way," polite conversation could only go so far. Eventually, I would steer the discussion back to the reason I was there.

"So is there anything I can do for you guys? Do you feel like eating yet? Can I get you a Gatorade or protein shake to drink? I can even run over to Burger King and get you a Whopper and some fries," I'd offer hopefully.

They grew tired of that predictable turn in the dialogue fast. That was usually when the conversation would be over. One day, Ajmal shook his head and said calmly but firmly, "Don't come back. Just don't come back. We're done hearing your lies. We're done talking."

I hadn't done anything for them since we'd met other than try to end their hunger strike with weak promises to see what I could do about their demand to get moved. As lame as that was, it was more than anyone else had done. Almost all the other people whom they had talked to had laughed off the notion that they could be housed anywhere other than segregation. Still, they could tell I had no more intention than anyone else of getting them moved, and they knew I didn't have the authority either.

When they told me not to come back, that was it. I hadn't officially failed yet because the prisoners were still alive, but they weren't eating, so that status could change any day. I continued to work my jobs with TA2 and COIN, but in the back of my mind, I was nervous that the next call I got would be that one or all three of the prisoners had succumbed to starvation.

A couple of days after Ajmal had dismissed me, my CW sent me to medical. Haji, Ajmal, and Delawar had been taken there because of their weakened conditions and were being provided nourishment intravenously. They were still segregated from the rest of the population, so the three of them were in a private area of the hospital, in individual cells separated from the other patients. They didn't look good at all, and my first thought when I saw them was how far downhill they'd gone in only a few days. I tried to sound upbeat when I spoke.

"You guys are so serious about this! You really are going to do it, aren't you?"

Delawar didn't even acknowledge my presence, but Ajmal nodded weakly and told me again, "We are prepared to go all the way."

I looked around at their medical cells. The segregation rooms in medical were practically identical to the ones they'd spent the last few years in. They were separated from one another, each cell side by side. There were mats to sleep on and blankets to keep warm, and they were allowed to have books if they wanted them. Like the segregation cells, the ones in medical had open ceilings covered in steel mesh too.

"You guys have everything you need," I said. "You even get a few things you want."

Ajmal shook his head.

"We want to be out of segregation. We want to be with other people—with our people."

What could I do? I couldn't watch them die over the issue of where they spent their detention. That was when I promised to move them. Even with my superiors impressing on me that those three were never to be moved, I promised them that we would work on it, not that I'd "see what I could do" but an actual promise that I would change their situation. They didn't buy it at first. Ajmal grew agitated, and with all the strength he could muster, sat up and told me how little faith they had in anything an American had to say.

"We listen to you guys' bullshit all the time, your Colonel Braswell and General Eggers," he said, making it clear that they'd talked with our top officers and hadn't gotten anywhere. "Nothing ever changes, and no one will ever allow us to be moved."

"I promise," I said, looking Ajmal right in the eye. "I'll move you. I'll start today looking into what we need to do."

After a beat, something in Ajmal's face relaxed, and his eyes softened the smallest bit. I knew then that I'd made progress and should take advantage of it before the moment passed.

"You need to drink," I said, holding my breath.

Ajmal said something to Haji who made a sound of assent.

"Yes?" I asked.

"Yes." Ajmal nodded.

I had the medical attendant bring them each a little can of Ensure. We popped the tops and they drank, and the hunger strike was officially over. Just that fast. It wasn't only these three that were involved though. Many of the other prisoners had taken on their cause, not because they wanted to be moved but mostly because they wanted to react to something. There were still guys on the Afghan side of the facility who would take a day or so off from eating so they could get placed on the hunger strike list, then they would eat just enough to keep from going to medical. With the number of detainees that were involved in Haji's hunger strike, that crazy cycle was the only reason medical wasn't wall-to-wall with prisoners hooked up to IVs.

"Give me the word," I said to Ajmal. "Tell me what to tell the other guys to let them know the strike is over, and it's okay to eat."

He conferred for a moment with Haji, calling to him over the wall. After Haji responded, Ajmal asked for a piece of paper and something to write with. I quickly handed over the pen and small notebook I always carried. Ajmal carefully wrote out a couple of lines in Arabic, then handed them back to me and indicated that I was to give them to Haji for his signature.

"Take this note to the other side. When the others see what it says, everything will be okay," Ajmal said.

When I went over to the ANA side and delivered the message, it was like magic. Everyone drank or ate a little food, Ensure was delivered by the case for those who'd gone the longest without nourishment, and the hunger strike was officially over. It was the hardest one I'd ever worked on and the most stressful. Sure there was the understanding of how those men ended up at Sabalu Harrison, but they were still humans, and we didn't want anything to happen to them. It had taken weeks instead of hours or minutes to diffuse this strike, but I was amazed at how quickly things turned around, how simply it seemed to have been resolved.

The truth was, at that point, all I had done was restart the clock. I'd promised to get the three prisoners moved out of segregation, so if that didn't happen, they would strike again, and the next time, there would be nothing I could do to convince them to end it. When I made my report to the CW, I had to outline what had taken place and how I'd ended the strike, and he responded by saying out loud what I was already thinking.

"When they find out you can't do what you said you'd do, this is all going to start again."

"Well, it gives us some breathing room," I said.

Back in my room, I thought over what I'd gotten myself into. Yeah, I'd bought a little time by promising to do something that wasn't likely to happen. But what was the worst-case scenario? The detainees would go along for a few weeks, eating and drinking. Then in the end, they might start another hunger strike. They would have regained their strength, so even then, we would still have a little time before they ended up in medical again. However, at that point, they would consider me a liar, exactly like everyone else they'd talked to. I determined that wouldn't happen. They wouldn't resume the strike and wind up back in medical because I would actually find a way to get them moved, whatever it took.

CHAPTER 8

Ajmal, Haji, and Delawar had to be kept in the medical until their health improved. They remained there under monitoring for five days. Haji had been feeling unwell prior to ending the hunger strike, but they all recovered fairly quickly. With the belief that I would have them moved to the other side of the facility—if not directly from medical, at least shortly after the doctor released them—they drank all the Gatorade and Ensure the medical assistants brought them, making a show of swallowing to demonstrate that their part of the bargain was complete. It didn't take long before they were back on solid food. Haji started feeling better, and all three detainees were in good spirits too, anticipating finally getting what they had wanted for so long.

For my part, I kept my finger on the pulse, looking in on all three regularly and asking how they were doing. Even if all I got was a nod, that was positive feedback that reassured me that the dialogue was still open between us. When I visited, however, I tried to keep the talk away from the specifics of how I was going to accomplish what I'd promised.

"Let me worry about that," I'd say. "You guys just work on getting your health back."

Before things had gotten bad enough to put them in medical, I had occasionally asked my CW and higher-ups about moving the three prisoners out of segregation. I would talk to a different person each time in hopes that I'd hit the jackpot and find someone who wasn't stubbornly determined to keep those specific prisoners in segregation, and each time, I was basically told the same thing: "Under no circumstances are those three to be moved. They are to stay where they are at."

No matter who I talked to, they left no margin for misinterpretation. After my intel contact had fully briefed me about who the three detainees were, I could see why moving them was such a big deal. Any other time in my military career, I would have followed the orders and left the prisoners in segregation without giving it another thought, but this time was different for more than one reason, although those reasons were interrelated.

First, this was the one time I hadn't been able to diffuse a hunger strike within minutes. The issue with that was more than ego. It also had to do with the fact that my failure to end the hunger strike quickly had led to the prisoners' lives being jeopardized—the second reason I couldn't give up on the idea of getting them moved out of segregation. Third, I had given them my word that I would get them moved, and that was something I wasn't willing to sacrifice. The promise wasn't made impulsively. It was true that I hadn't thought the plan through to the point of figuring out how I would pull it off, but I had meant it when I promised to move them.

A plan started to take shape in my mind, and I began looking around the US side of the detention facility to see if we had any empty cells large enough for my purposes. My idea was not to put them into a cell with thirty other detainees but instead, place them in one that was big enough to house all three of them. Ideally, it would be one with an empty cell on either side of it to keep them from communicating with other prisoners nearby. That way, they would be together instead of solitary and alone in separate cells, but they wouldn't be in a general-population situation where they could easily interact with and influence other prisoners. I figured that would satisfy their stipulation to be together, but they would still be in US custody.

Unfortunately, there weren't any cells on the US side that would work. Either the size was too large or too small, or there weren't empty cells next to them to create a buffer. Next, I went over to the Afghan side of the prison to see what accommodations were available over there. By then, the status and reputation I'd built up afforded me the ability to freely move from one side to the other, often without taking someone with me, so I could look around at their cells virtually unsupervised. If any of the larger ones were empty, I thought I might be able to swing a sort of compromise to get Haji, Ajmal, and Delawar moved to the ANA side.

All I had to do to make good on my word was to move Haji and his friends. I even considered transferring them to an entirely empty house if one was available. After all, Parwan Detention Facility is a big place. Eventually, I found an empty cell on the ANA side that was perfect for my plan. It was large enough for three men, and it had empty cells on either side of it. I went back to my desk on the US side and sent a request upstairs. In it, I outlined how the three detainees had initiated a hunger strike that eventually gained enough momentum to include over one hundred people and that they had only one demand: to be moved out of segregation. I pointed out that if these three detainees were not moved, they were capable of creating a nightmare situation in the form of riots, hunger strikes, etc., and that they'd already shown their influence stretched to every house in the facility. I knew circumstances like those would leave us in total chaos with pretty much no way out. I had said I'd move them, but I wouldn't have any credibility if it didn't happen, so who would talk our military out of that mess?

In the second part of my request, I explained that I had located an empty cell on the ANA side of Sabalu Harrison that was large enough to house all three detainees together, avoiding putting them in with other prisoners while going along with their mandate to be moved. I pointed out that there were empty "buffer" cells on either side and that they would still be in a situation that would make it fairly easy to monitor them, fulfilling the US requirement of retaining custody of the three prisoners.

That last part was the biggest hurdle I faced, though I didn't know it. At the time, I was aware that usually, once the US turned someone over to the Afghanis on the other side of the facility, we would have to take our hands off of them. For that reason, we always wanted to know for a fact that anyone being released to the ANA was not a terrorist because odds were they could end up going free, especially if they had the money to buy their way out. I wasn't fluent with the system at that point, however, so that was the one small but important detail I didn't understand. I realized that what we did know for a fact about the three detainees was that they had ties to the Taliban and the Haqqani Network and were involved in terrorist activities in the past, but I figured we could keep as good an eye on them on the other side as we did in segregation. It wasn't clear to me that who they were was the huge red flag that had kept them where they were up to that point.

Naturally, when the answer to my request came back, it wasn't favorable: absolutely not. It's not going to happen. It wasn't a big surprise to me, but I had held out one last hope that I could get things done through conventional channels.

I'd been hoping that my request wouldn't be blocked, though it would be easy enough to pass the buck and tell Ajmal that Haji was right, that the powers that be had said no. That might get me off the hook with them, but it would certainly damage my credibility. That's why, while I was waiting for a response to my request, I'd been working on a plan B which I set into motion the day before the detainees were to be released from medical. I had the Afghanis create an order that stipulated that once the doctor had okayed them to be released from medical, they were to be moved into the new cell I'd found for them on the ANA side. Once again, the confidence and good will I'd built up came in handy, and they didn't question me about whether anyone on the US side had okayed the directive. When I handed the orders to the staff in medical, they asked, "Is this okay with your people?"

"Hey, I *am* my people!" I replied confidently.

With the ANA guards standing on either side of me nodding their heads, what else could the doctors do but release the three prisoners into our custody?

The actual physical act of moving them was almost as difficult and involved as getting the orders had been. Whenever a prisoner was moved from one place to another inside Sabalu Harrison, they had to wear blacked-out goggles so they couldn't see where they were going and were placed in a wheelchair to make it impossible for them to count steps. Since they also couldn't see through the goggles, it kept them from knowing where they were inside the facility. We had to go through that process with all three, but they were securely locked away behind the door of their new shared cell by ten o'clock that night. It wasn't exactly what they'd requested, but it was enough to satisfy them.

Unfortunately, my victory was short-lived. By six the next morning, the general was aware of the move, and he personally came to the prison to get things straightened out. Everyone in the vicinity knew exactly how upset he was.

"Who did this?" the general demanded. "What the fuck is going on here? This is *not* happening. I want these fucking people back in their fucking cells now!"

And that quickly, everything was reversed.

My CW pulled me into his office and closed the door.

"Ooohhh, man. This is bad," he said.

Inside, I was dying, nervous as hell that I would go down for what I'd pulled. I tried to stay cool and confident on the outside though, acting like I didn't know I was the reason the general was upset.

"What's the problem? I ran my idea past you."

"Yeah, and I told you those guys needed to stay where they were at," he retorted, understandably wanting to avoid the slightest bit of responsibility, "At least until the six-thirty-sixth leaves."

"You said they *probably* should stay where they were at," I said, nitpicking words to cover my own ass. The truth was that as he'd grown more comfortable with letting me handle the other hunger strikes my way, his attitude had become one of "I'm telling you not to do that, but I'm not watching you every minute of the day, so…" In essence, ask no questions; hear no lies. I had taken that as permission to do what I had to do to get things done.

"Look, it ended the hunger strike," I told him. "Promising to get those guys moved wasn't enough. That only put things on hold. They trusted me enough to take a drink and end the strike, but they told me that if I didn't make good on that promise, they would start again. If I hadn't come through, they would never have trusted me again. It was a chance, but I had to take it."

"They'll be moved back," the CW said, shaking his head. "The general is taking care of that right now."

"That's fine. They already don't like you guys. They're not gonna respond to you no matter what you do. They don't trust you, and if they start another hunger strike, they'll die in your custody, and you know you can't have that. It had to be this way."

What could my CW say? He knew I was right. It was a last-ditch play, but I'd taken the chance. What I'd done had earned the detainees' trust and ended one of the biggest hunger strikes they'd had to deal with at Sabalu Harrison. The CW threw his hands in the air, defeated.

The general's rampage lasted a couple of hours that morning. He took it to the ANA side of the facility too, but no one over there claimed to know where the orders originated. Over and over again, the general was told, "We don't know what's going on. We were never consulted about this." Somehow, my name never came up, at least to my knowledge. No one other than my CW ever talked to me about the incident, and I was never reprimanded for it. It's possible that my CW and others up the chain of command were aware of what was going on and simply chose to play their parts. It was a win/win to allow the move so I could end the hunger strike, while the command claimed they knew nothing about it, which is completely plausible. I was left out of the loop though, so either way, it was more divine intervention as far as I was concerned.

So in the space of less than ten hours, I had moved Haji, Ajmal, and Delawar out of segregation, and the general had moved them back. As expected, they were furious. However, their anger was directed at everyone but me. Later that day, once they were back in segregation, I went to visit them, and Haji immediately started talking to Ajmal, who had to speak fast to keep up while translating the conversation.

"You've done something for me that no one else has done for me," the old man said. "You did what you said. I have talked with General Burns, and he doesn't like me. Colonel Paulsen, all the others, they're not going to do me any favors. I've been here for four years, and the colonel is the one who told me they're going to leave me here the rest of my life."

Suddenly, though my brilliant plan had ultimately failed, I saw it was a beginning. It opened dialogue, and all the months of breaking up riots and getting shit thrown at us from the cells, working on things for COIN, collecting information every day, and the work all the guys in my unit contributed to free me up to do this third job— all of that was now in the background, secondary to the connection I'd made with these three.

In all the time I'd spent talking to Ajmal and communicating with Haji through him, Delawar hadn't said a word directed at me, and his rare acknowledgment of my presence was typically a hateful glare. Usually, he would sit silently during our meetings, hardly moving and just being intimidating. That day, he was up and walking around his cell with his hands behind his back or standing at the door of his cell, stroking his beard and looking thoughtful. He didn't say anything then either, but he was obviously listening and very much engaged in what was going on.

Seeing that complete change in Delawar, I knew everything was going to be okay. It gave me back the confidence I'd temporarily lost, so I jumped right in, putting myself on their side.

"Look, I'm really sorry," I told them. "I'll get this reversed. I don't know what the problem is, but I'll get the general to move you back, and I'll even get him to apologize."

My bravado worked. The three were stunned by my announcement.

"No—how can you do that?" Haji asked through Ajmal.

"Leave it to me," I said. "I'll get it done, just give me time."

I'd already shown that I was a man of my word, so they fully expected that I could get them out of segregation again and for good this time. Still, that act of good faith hadn't earned me a blank check. I couldn't put them off indefinitely. To keep another hunger strike from starting, they would have to be moved again soon.

CHAPTER 9

Although the detainees trusted me now, they still wanted to know that I was working on getting them out of segregation and that they were my top priority. It seemed like every twenty minutes they were demanding to see me. I'd get called in to see them for trivial things. I would walk in, and Ajmal would say, "We don't want juice with our meal, could we get something else?" and I'd say, "Sure," then I'd turn to the guards and say, "Get this guy milk instead of juice." It empowered them. Someone was listening to them, and it fed their egos.

It was little things like that, but I remained patient. That contact several times throughout the day helped strengthen our rapport. Because part of my job was to try to obtain information from the detainees, no one saw it as a problem for me to visit those particular prisoners frequently or to spend several hours at a time with them. The general didn't ever say anything about it, and when the new MP brigade arrived, my new CW was as supportive as his predecessor, maybe even more so. He'd been back briefed on everything going on, and by then, those up the chain of command felt I had a grip on what was happening. Since everyone was cool with it, I kept doing what I was doing. I would schedule time to check in with Haji and the others every other day, but they would usually send word on the days in between that they wanted to talk. I never knew when they might share an important piece of information, so I'd usually end up visiting with them daily.

Most of the time, they just wanted to talk and didn't reveal any useful information. The majority of the time, they were only looking to get attention and interaction that they didn't normally get. Those days, Haji would talk about his business back home or his kids, things you might expect any old man to reminisce about. I spent hours and hours listening, alert for any small nugget of information that could mean something or be useful.[iv]

We had never talked about their involvement with the Taliban or their ties to the Haqqani Network before they'd been sent to medical. Once they were back in segregation, however, I let them know that I had been made aware of their backgrounds, that I knew why they were in Sabalu Harrison and what they'd been accused of. The interesting thing about Haji, Ajmal, and Delawar was that they never denied who they were or what they did when they talked to me. Other prisoners I'd come in contact with at the facility were a lot like ones I deal with in civilian life. They had that classic denial thing going on and would insist that they'd been falsely accused and had done nothing. These three, on the other hand, were very matter-of-fact about their past and seemed to have accepted the fact that they would never leave the Parwan Detention Facility.

From the time I'd first met the three detainees, our visits were conducted with cell doors between us. Even when I went to see them in medical, they were in segregated cells. That got old fast, especially on the days when our meetings would last four or five hours. We couldn't continue communicating that way for long if I were going to retain their trust and confidence, so things had to go to the next level at some point. I was still trying to figure out how I could get them permanently moved out of segregation, so I thought maybe getting them out of their cells when we talked might temporarily placate them and buy a little more time.

One day when I arrived, I didn't take a seat on the folding chair the guard had fetched for me. Instead, I asked Ajmal, "If I bring all of you into another room, will you be compliant?"

He had been at Sabalu Harrison long enough to know that I was asking if all three of them would act appropriately and not try to pull anything if I were to take them out of their cells.

Ajmal translated my question for the other two, and all three nodded at me eagerly. I was confident in the connection I'd made with them, so I'd already had a classroom on the base prepared for the occasion, with chai and pillows on the floor for seating. Two guards helped me get the detainees blindfolded and seated in wheelchairs. Then we took them on a little vacation from segregation for the afternoon.

When we got to the classroom, we removed the goggles, and I invited the detainees to have a seat on the cushions. Then I told the guards they could step outside. Even Ajmal, Haji, and Delawar were surprised at that, and the guards warily glanced at the three of them, free and seated on pillows, enjoying cups of tea.

"Are you sure you want to sit in a room with these guys and no guards?" one of them asked.

"I'm fine. Everyone, just go away," I said, knowing they would be nearby if I needed them.

Once we were alone, Ajmal couldn't resist asking, "Aren't you afraid to be with us if we're not restrained?"

Truthfully, every time I interacted with those three, I was waiting for them to make their move. I would remind myself of the possibility that they had shanks or might attempt a pile-up attack. It would be quite the coup to harm or kill a member of the US guard force inside his own facility. Word would get out fast and give momentum to an uprising or worse, so we always had to be very conscious of the possibilities. There was a protocol though. We were always to be cordial and be professional but expect the worst from the men we were interviewing. I was on alert at all times, so whether or not I was afraid didn't matter.[v] The only thing that did was what I let them believe, so I laughed and said, "Of course not!"

I took a seat and asked if the tea met with their approval. They all smiled and nodded. After taking a sip, Haji spoke, and Ajmal translated.

"We know what you want."

This was something they would say now and then during the course of a conversation, but I hadn't figured out what they thought I wanted. That day, my response was very much like every other time they'd brought up the topic.

"I don't know what you mean. What do I want? I'm here to make sure you guys are happy, healthy, and eating."

Ajmal smiled but shook his head.

"We know that's bullshit. We know you want information."

In the past, they'd dropped the subject when I appeared to play dumb, so this was the most we'd ever talked about what I supposedly wanted from them. I went along with it.

"So what information do I want?" I asked.

"You want to know about the sergeant."

I have to admit to losing my composure for a split second. In my head, I was thinking, *Does he really mean* that *sergeant? He couldn't mean Bergdahl!* Keeping my face as impassive as I could manage, I stuttered a little when I replied, "Well, I-I'm not here for that. I'm here to make sure you guys are okay."

Ajmal smiled knowingly and changed the subject. We were playing a game, and it had just gotten interesting. The detainees had made a calculated move to let me know that they had information about the American soldier who was being held prisoner by the Taliban. I had no way of knowing whether that information was important or not and could only assume that it might be, but my job was to gather and report intel, and this was the biggest thing I'd come across since arriving in Afghanistan. I was dying to say "Tell me everything you know!" but I had to play it cool. I couldn't let them know I was interested in what they had to say. All I could do was wait for them to bring up "the sergeant" again and see what other information they might share.

When I made my report to the CW after that visit, I was surprised that he wasn't as enthusiastic as I was about the information the three detainees could have.

"These guys have been here for four years," he said. "Anything they have to say is old news."

I supposed that was true, but to me, it was brand-new information, and we were talking about a POW. If there was anything I could do to help, I wanted to do it. All my reports were sent upstairs for analysis and review, so I waited until I figured everyone up the chain of command was aware of what had happened. When I asked my CW about it again, he told me in very clear terms not to pursue it.

"Stay in your own lane, Herbert. Mind your own business and work on your own stuff. There are people working on that. We know who Haji is, and we know what he knows. Just leave it at that."

I realized that ever since word had gone out that the Taliban had Bowe Bergdahl, everyone from the CIA to the NSA was working on finding him and getting him back. They'd talked to everyone in the prisons who were associated with the Taliban or any terrorist organization, painstakingly taking note of any small scrap of information, like miners panning for gold. Considering Haji's standing in the Haqqani Network, it was safe to say that numerous people from a variety of agencies had talked to him over and over, going through the whole cycle of interview and interrogation repeatedly. It was understandable that they believed they'd gotten all they were going to get out of him. What's more, they probably thought I was going to mess up the whole operation by asking questions that somebody else had already asked. I know I would be the same way. In my civilian job, I prefer anyone not involved to stay away from any investigation I am working on.

The more I thought about it though, the more I fixated on it. Part of it was natural human curiosity, but more than that, I felt like I had an obligation to learn as much as I could from the prisoners, collect whatever could be collected. Maybe it was old information that had already been picked over, but maybe there was one new detail, however small, that had been missed the first time around. It wasn't that I thought I could do better than everyone before me; it just didn't sit right with me to stand down. These guys knew about the POW, and getting information like that was my mission. If I could find out anything new or shed light on something that had been previously overlooked, that could be the key to bringing Bowe Bergdahl home.

What if it were my son? What if I knew for a fact that someone could help him, but they didn't because they'd been told to back off? Knowing that my son wants to be in the military someday made the matter a personal one, and those were the thoughts that echoed through my mind. They drove my decision to pursue the issue. I worried that if I turned away now, I would condemn the guy to be a hostage for the rest of his life. On the other hand, going for it might result in a piece of information that would help locate and free him. I hoped that someone would do that for me if I were in the same situation. Either way, I wanted to be a good sailor and do the best job that I could. If he's found, if he's not found, whatever happened, I did what I could do, and my conscience would be clear. One thing was for sure: that was the end of any good sleep I got while in Afghanistan.

CHAPTER 10

As time passed, and the three prisoners remained in segregation, they became more and more convinced that I wouldn't be able to move them again. I had my doubts too because I was hitting a dead end with each new idea I had. I wanted them to know that I was still trying to find a solution and that I had all the confidence in the world that it would happen, but it would take time. Meanwhile, I continued to look for ways to maintain and strengthen their trust in me and build the relationship. The way I treated them enhanced the rapport we had, and Haji agreed to do a few favors for the US military if it was me doing the asking.

The best example was when the prisoners would riot or start a hunger strike. Usually, the detainees would act up as a way to call attention to an issue and get what they wanted, like fresh dates and nuts for a traditional holiday or if they wanted a special kind of juice. They might feel like they didn't get enough food, or they might want more towels. Religious views were a big motivation too, so sometimes they would revolt when people from opposing tribes were put into a cell together. The detainees would use any excuse to throw feces or urine at the US guard force or try to attack them from behind bars.

The protocol to diffuse those situations was to bring the mullahs from each house into one room to find out what was going on. Mullahs are educated in Muslim religious law and trained in Muslim traditions, much like a priest or cleric in a Christian religion. They are important in the Muslim lifestyle in general, but they play an especially significant part inside a detainment facility since providing each house with a mullah ensures the detainees can practice their faith. When there was trouble, we would bring the mullahs together and negotiate with them, conceding to some demands and, in other instances, threatening to take away comforts and privileges if the prisoners didn't knock it off and straighten up. The mullahs would deliver the message, but it would often take more than one meeting before things settled down and got back to normal.

That all changed once Haji got involved. During our conversations, he would hint at the status he'd earned because of his involvement with the Haqqani Network. He wasn't boastful; he was simply stating facts about how well-known he was inside and outside the walls of the Parwan Detention Facility. One day, while a violent disturbance was going on in one of the houses that experienced issues almost daily, I asked him, "If you talked to the mullahs, could you get this trouble to stop?"

When he told me that of course, he could, I had a follow-up question.

"Will you do it?"

Haji thought about it for a moment, then agreed, so we put the goggles on him, placed him in a wheelchair, and took him to the house that was rioting. When we wheeled him in, stopping in front of the first six cells so he could deliver his message, we learned that Haji was every bit the person he said he was. People actually did know him. It was like Elvis was in the building. As a favor to me, he told the mullahs in those front cells that things needed to settle down, and they passed the word on throughout the house. I don't speak Pashto, but I had no problem understanding Haji's final words: "No more, no more."

The next day, the place was like a library. The prisoners were on their very best behavior with no demands having been met. No second and third meetings with the mullahs and no negotiating. Being able to subdue an entire house gave me a lot of power and control. It was something no one else could do, not even the whole guard force combined, and Haji wouldn't talk to the mullahs for anyone but me.

Of course, Haji got something out of it too. He got to spend time outside of his cell, so seeing that was another thing I could do for him, that reinforced his trust in me and helped strengthen our rapport, I would sometimes take him for a wheelchair ride. He had picked up some English, though he chose not to let on to most of the US guard force that he could understand, and he rarely spoke to me in English, preferring to have Ajmal translate for him. Still, it allowed for conversations on our outings, even if I did most of the talking.

Over time, as Haji helped me more and more by talking to the mullahs, I would comp him little luxuries that he hadn't previously had. Sometimes I'd pick up food from Burger King and take it to Haji and his two friends when I visited them. Other times, we would do a deal for lotion. Haji's skin would get dry, but the prisoners weren't allowed to keep lotion in their cells, so he would talk to a house and get it calmed down, and I would get him some lotion along with a memo saying he was allowed to keep it and that it was to be resupplied when he ran out. That way, the guards couldn't confiscate it as contraband. One time, we made a deal for a watch. Haji had talked about wishing he had a way of knowing when it was time for prayer. So the next time he helped me deal with a rioting house, I got him a watch that had an alarm on it that he could set to go off when it was time to pray. Getting things like that and being able to keep them usually took the act of a general, so it was a small favor on my part that made it possible to get things done simply with a memo to the guard force authorizing the detainees to keep their things.

Although the library at Sabalu Harrison was locked up, we were still supposed to allow the prisoners to have access to Qurans and other religious books. The US is very accommodating about allowing the International Committee of the Red Cross to come in and provide the detainees with Qurans and a variety of other things for them to read. The ICRC is a neutral organization, but it's favorable toward the prisoners, so members of the Red Cross also make it a point to check on specific prisoners and report back if a family member on the outside has inquired about them. They've been known to pass messages between detainees and their families but, typically, not anything subversive. Usually, it's simply news of someone's health or what's been happening back home or in the prison.

There is no set schedule for the ICRC to come in and pass out books, so there are times when they're not allowed in, like if the prisoners were being particularly difficult or unruly. If too much time passes between visits though, the prisoners start complaining that the Army is preventing them access to their religious books.

One day, the CW said, "The ICRC is coming in. They've been pushed away too many times recently. They're looking for Haji because they know he has been in medical. They want to see him and find out how he is doing so they can tell his family he's okay."

Of course, no one, not even from the Red Cross, can simply go into a detention facility unaccompanied by the military, so the CW told me I would be escorting one of the ICRC people around that day. I'm sure part of the assignment had to do with my relationship with Haji and his buddies. When we got around to his cell, he told the woman from the Red Cross that everything was great. He pointed to me and smiled as he told her how much he appreciated my help and the way I treated him. I figured she must have been keeping tabs on his circumstances for a while because she later thanked me for taking care of him, talking as if she knew him pretty well. I had no doubt that the report back to the family would be a favorable one.

As we were getting ready to leave the segregation house, Ajmal called out to me.

"Herbert! Can you stay and talk?"

I never knew when their talks would result in useful information or when it was only therapy for their boredom. However, since I was hoping to hear more about Bergdahl, I would make time for the three detainees whenever they asked.

"Sure," I told him. Hooking a thumb toward the woman from the Red Cross, I said, "I need to escort her back out, then I'll get a room set up so we can be comfortable."

I found an empty classroom and had a few pillows tossed onto the floor, then brought Ajmal, Haji, and Delawar in for a talk. When everyone was unblindfolded and seated comfortably, I asked, "So what can I do for you guys today?"

Ajmal looked to Haji, who nodded.

"What can *we* do for *you*?" Ajmal replied.

Somehow I knew that this was it. I hadn't asked about the sergeant after they first mentioned him. Showing any interest would have given them the upper hand. Besides, I'd been told not to pursue it. If they were offering me information though, I would be in the driver's seat, and no one could say that I'd disobeyed orders.

"Well, what can you tell me about the sergeant?" I asked as casually as I could.

They didn't give me the entire story that day, but they did open up. They seemed as eager to talk as I was to get information. Ajmal did most of the talking, of course, with Haji interjecting a detail once in a while and answering questions I asked. As usual, Delawar remained silent for the most part but paid close attention to everything that was said.

Through Ajmal, Haji told me that they had been among the group that had captured Bergdahl. I immediately thought that was a load of shit, but how could I really know? Maybe they were the ones who had picked him up in the desert. Everything they told me would go in my report anyway and be sent up the ladder to be analyzed and verified, so I just nodded, taking it all in.

They told me that the sergeant had tried to escape and that they had sold him after they'd had him for a short time. Much later, I found out that those details fit with Bergdahl's account, so in hindsight, what they told me that day could be true. The issue was that they did know a lot of information that wasn't common knowledge at the time which led me to believe that following up with them could lead somewhere. Unfortunately that day, as would happen often, the information stopped flowing as suddenly as it had started before they revealed where he was. I was sure that the people holding Bergdahl would move him frequently, but these three guys seemed confident that they knew where he was, and they assured me that he was alive. Then out of the blue, that was it. Suddenly Haji was talking about his family and asking about mine, and we were off subject.

That's how it went over the next couple of months, with many more conversations about mundane topics occurring than ones about the sergeant. What's more, the flow of information slowed considerably. Not only would I have to wait weeks before they would bring up the subject again, but more often than not, I would only get one small bit of information at a time. It drove me crazy, but I could understand their motivation. The information on Bergdahl was the only thing they had going for them. It was their golden ticket. Once they let it go, they'd be done, doomed to spend the rest of their days in segregation with no attention, nothing to do, and no one to talk to. It was likely they would never get any kind of attention again. At least with valuable information, those three frequently got out of their cells, and the little perks I furnished sweetened the deal.

One issue I couldn't completely discount was that they were setting me up. They had all the time in the world on their hands and nothing to do. It was more than possible that their motives for feeding me nuggets of information on Bergdahl had nothing to do with helping the sergeant or me. When training for this job, I'd learned that more times than not, when a prisoner seemed to take a liking to you, it was because he was luring you in a position to make a mistake so he could use it against you. "I'm going to tell your guard force you brought me a hamburger unless you bring me a cell phone," for instance. In this case, I had permission to do everything I did for them, from the occasional hamburger to giving Haji a watch. Well, at least I had my CW's blessing to do what I had to do to get my job done. It was little things like that, but whenever I gave them anything at all, I always weighed out what the best possible outcome could be to determine whether it was worth the risk. Would getting them some lotion or other restricted item open the door for them to put the screws to me? Would they ask me to get them a cell phone or leave the doors unlocked? Or would it result in the final piece of the puzzle that would rescue Bowe Bergdahl? My curiosity, as well as my tunnel vision, kept me going down the path to see where it would lead.

To their credit, however, they never asked me to do anything illegal. They never put me in a jeopardizing position with my government, and I think it's because I had come through for them. The level of trust was surreal. At one point Haji said to me, "You've done more for me than anybody else has. I trust you like a brother. I would cut out my eyeball for you."

We also had many discussions about how hard it was to get things done.

"Your government is a pain in the ass," Haji would say, shaking his head. "They won't do anything. It takes forever to get anything done. Your government should allow you to do business for them, and I should do business for my government because we could get stuff done."

I had to agree with him to a point, but on the other hand, things weren't flowing as quickly with us as I would have liked. Through Ajmal, Haji would give me barely enough information to keep me interested, and sometimes, it wasn't even about Bergdahl. One day when I came to see them, instead of talking about the sergeant, Ajmal asked me if I knew about "the woman" that had been captured.

"What? What woman?" I asked, taken off guard.

Apparently, a couple had been taken hostage the previous year, an American woman and a Canadian man. After Ajmal had filled in some details, I remembered hearing about them. My understanding was that Caitlan Coleman and Joshua Boyle were on vacation and that Joshua had brought some paperwork with him that might have had something to do with the Taliban. I'm not sure what was written on the papers, but he wasn't necessarily a Taliban sympathizer. The story was that he thought if he had that manuscript with him, he and Caitlan would be allowed to hike around the country without being bothered. If that was really the plan, it didn't work out so great for them. The Taliban had grabbed them, and they were still being held. Haji told me several things that I later learned to be true, like the fact that Caitlan had kidney problems, and that she was pregnant. Haji thought that the couple were doing well, but didn't have much information on them, so that was all he shared about the American and the Canadian before our discussions turned back to Bergdahl.

After days of not talking about the sergeant, I acted skeptical when Ajmal mentioned him again.

"Is he even still alive?" I asked. "I mean, you're in here. Even if you were involved when he was first captured, how can you know whether or not they've kept him alive?"

These guys were connected. They could get any information they wanted from the outside. Their knowledge of my kids and where I came from was just one example of that. I hoped playing cynical would make them want to spill more information. When Ajmal assured me that Bergdahl was very much alive, I asked if proof of life could be provided.

"A proof of life video was made, don't you know about this?" he asked. When I told him that this was the first I was hearing about it, he said, "One was made but never sent because the talks stopped."

He was referring to the short-lived attempt to make a deal for Bergdahl's release. The Taliban had a list of twenty-four detainees being held at Guantanamo Bay whom they wanted released in exchange for Bowe Bergdahl. Many presidents and others in power have said they won't negotiate with terrorists, but it was the terrorists who refused to negotiate in this case. Essentially, they demanded we swap twenty-four specific detainees from Gitmo for Bergdahl, and although the US never wants to leave anyone behind, twenty-four for one wasn't an option, so naturally, our side tried to talk them down. No. They wouldn't have it. It was twenty-four or nothing, so the flag over Qatar that signified open dialogue came down, and talks hadn't resumed since.

"Where is this video? Can I get a copy of it?" I asked, trying to sound unconvinced instead of hopeful.

"Yes. Do you want it?" Haji asked through Ajmal. "As my friend, what will it do for you? Will it give you power?"

"No, it won't really do anything for me, but it will give hope to the sergeant's family. It will show the US that he is still alive." Then I asked, "So how can I get this video? Do you have someone on the outside who can mail it to me?"

"Do you have an email address?"

"Yes, I do," I replied, surprised.

"We will talk," he said, indicating the three of them would need to discuss things before going any further. "Then we will have the video sent to you."

Now we were starting to get somewhere. After months of dropping small bits of information like breadcrumbs, the detainees had finally given me something that could be useful. If we could get our hands on a video of Bergdahl, we might be able to trace where it came from. Our experts could study it for clues as to where he was, at least at the time the video was made. The terrain (if visible in the video), background noises, anything could point to a specific area, and our guys could pick up his trail and possibly find him. Plus, a video would show the Bergdahl family and the world that Bowe was still alive.

CHAPTER 11

For a while, our meetings were scheduled for certain days, but as the detainees opened up more and more about the sergeant, that changed. Each meeting was a step closer to finding Bowe. I started to look forward to our conversations and began dropping in on the three prisoners between scheduled meetings. I would go to my regular job, attend meetings, and make sure my responsibilities were taken care of. Then after dinner, I would walk a couple of miles to the segregation house to see Haji, Ajmal, and Delawar. Many times, I would be lying in bed, unable to sleep, and would get up and go talk to them.

Every time I met with those three, I had to report to the CW of the intel unit everything we'd discussed. A lot of the time, I would simply send him an email, but whether it was my emails printed out or an actual report I'd typed, everything was sent "upstairs" for review. Even though initially I had been told to back off, the agencies with initials (CIA, NSA, etc.) sat up and took notice once the prisoners started talking about a proof-of-life video of Bergdahl. Those bureaus and organizations had been using all of their resources to find him for almost four years. They'd talked to Haji. They'd used different angles, and they'd come to a dead end, both in the search for Bowe and in negotiations to free him.

One afternoon, I got a call from an investigator with a federal agency.

"Petty Officer Herbert, this is Peter Siaperas," said the man on the other end of the line. "I understand you've been getting some intriguing information from a detainee in segregation."

"Yes, sir," I replied.

"We're very interested in what you're getting. You seem to have a rapport with this guy, and he seems to want to talk to you. Would you like to continue to talk to him?"

That was a surprise. After being told to stay in my lane, now this investigative agency wanted *me* to work with *them*? I had always figured everyone they had at their disposal was working day and night to bring Bergdahl home. At least, that's what I'd hoped, but I didn't know all the details of the paths they'd gone down in their search. However, the fact that top-level agencies, the all-stars of the game by all accounts, were working on the problem was pretty impressive. Of course I wanted to be in on that.

"I am always interested in helping," I replied. "What would it entail? What are my obligations? What's your idea of how this plays out?"

"Well, it looks like you're making good progress with what you're already doing," he said. "I can't tell you how to talk to this guy or how to do your job. We'd just like you to keep doing what you've been doing. Just let them talk. Stay on their good side. Keep their confidence in you. Do it however you've done it all along, and let's see how far you can take this."

What I had been doing was trading small favors, but the ultimate expectation from the three detainees was that they would be moved again and, this time, permanently. Maybe if I could do that, or at least if it appeared that a move was going to happen, that would speed up the flow of information. The next time I visited the prisoners, I raised the topic.

"So I've still been working on getting you moved back to the other side, and I think we have some options, but they'll take a little more time," I told them. "One idea is to wait for the 636th Battalion to mobilize and make the move then."

I'd heard talk that the 636th would be leaving, and a new Army brigade would be taking their place. It seemed like that in-between time when the next unit was coming in and setting up their own administration would be a good time to get the ANA to order another move. The detainees were a step ahead of me.

"The 636 is getting ready to leave soon. It will happen within weeks," Ajmal told me.

"Well, if they're leaving, let's just wait. I'll move you out when they're gone," I said, trying to hide my surprise at how well-informed he was. Apparently, Haji and his boys were better connected than I was.

"Give me a couple of weeks, and we'll get you out of here."

I didn't want to give them a specific date because number one, I didn't know exactly when the 636th was leaving, and number two, although I was going to try it, I wasn't sure the same trick I'd used before would work again. The detainees didn't push me to set a date, but they were obviously very capable of getting the information they wanted, so I knew I was back on the clock to get them moved and prevent another major hunger strike.

It was enough to boost their confidence in me though and to get them talking about the sergeant again. They didn't reveal anything new that day, but Haji started talking once more about how much I'd done for him and how he considered me a brother.

"When we get out, when you are done with your work here, we should meet," he said through Ajmal.

It was intriguing that after telling me the US would never let him go, Haji wanted to make plans to get together in the future. I'd spent months building a relationship with the three of them, but our meetings had always been in a manageable environment. Even when I had the guards leave the room, they were always within shouting distance if the prisoners tried to pull something. I'd never once considered staying in touch with Haji or any of them, and the thought of having a reunion with them was bizarre. Still, I had to maintain the relationship I'd forged, so balking at meeting with them wasn't an option.

"Sure. We'll always be friends. We should meet and stay in touch," I told them sarcastically.

Since I was the one who brought up the move again, I had to start laying the groundwork. I tried to keep an ear out for information on the 636th leaving but wasn't able to find out exactly when it was going to happen. The military guarded information like that closely, not wanting any of it to get out because of OPSEC. If the Taliban or other terrorist groups caught wind of specific times and dates that a unit was leaving, they could try to bomb the plane with hundreds of US soldiers on it. Because of that risk, it was paramount not to let that information slip out. Still, each unit only stayed at Bagram for about a year, so anyone could estimate when a unit might be leaving. Because of that, Ajmal's information was as accurate as it could be. All the news I could gather repeatedly pointed to two to three weeks. That meant finding another large cell on the Afghan side of the facility and getting it prepared to house three detainees. It would have to be inspected from corner to corner and floor to ceiling before. Sometimes the prisoners would pull threads from their blankets and tie things like a message or razor to one end and drop it down the drain, securing the other end to the metal cover over the drain so they or someone else could retrieve it later. Everything would be checked and rechecked and certified spotless before my detainees could move in. Even so, this time, knowing the concerns that had kept the three prisoners in segregation, I looked for a communal cell that was close to the US side and the intel offices. I found one that was regularly frequented by both ANA and US guard forces, and there were several cameras in the area too.

In the meantime, I'd started sharing information with the agencies that were involved. At one point, I told him about the first time I had moved the detainees and that the general had reversed it and moved them back.

"They've been patiently waiting for me to move them again," I said, referring to Haji and the other two. "I have a place for them, but I don't have a day and time yet. With your help though, we can make this happen sooner than later, and it would help our cause for sure."

Siaperas listened as I explained that the new cell was close and under surveillance, making it more secure than the general population or the previous cell I'd moved them to. Surprisingly, he was open to it.

"If this continues to be productive, would your people promote the move? I can talk to the general a few more times before he leaves," he offered.

The possibility of legitimately moving Haji, Ajmal, and Delawar was encouraging. Siaperas could see that a move was the deal maker and breaker for them. Anyone else who had been working with the three could have moved them a year or two before I got there. It was clear that the people who could have done that for them had drawn a line and decided that was one of the things that would never happen. Now, however, someone in power could make it happen. Of course, once moved, we would never take our leash off them. We would retain jurisdiction over those particular detainees, but it was a relief to know that there was a chance to come through for them again and that it might be a little easier than the last time.

Once more, things seemed to be almost effortlessly falling into place. Once Agent Siaperas was on board, getting the prisoners moved was suddenly being talked about openly. Sooner than expected, Siaperas let me know that a meeting had been scheduled to discuss moving forward and that he was pushing to have the three detainees housed together to generate momentum. When I shared the news with Haji, Ajmal, and Delawar, naturally, they were pleased, and it had the effect we were all hoping for. Information started flowing more regularly, and it started to look like there was a possibility of Sergeant Bergdahl going home sometime soon.

CHAPTER 12

Meeting with Haji and his friends face-to-face had become regular practice for our scheduled interviews. I would still drop in on them frequently in segregation, but they would be moved to a classroom furnished with pillows for official meetings. Sitting with those guys was both terrifying and satisfying at the same time. I had to always be on my guard with them and not be fooled by their supposed acts of kindness. For all I knew, any and all benevolent words and favors from them were attempts to lure me in a position of vulnerability. I prayed to God many times for the right words to say and the patience to complete this task.[vi] Although I could never fully relax when I was with the detainees, I always had a feeling that everything was going to be okay.

One evening when I entered the room, it became apparent that it wasn't likely to be one of our more productive discussions, at least as far as Bowe Bergdahl was concerned. After pleasant greetings, all smiles and handshakes, I was invited to sit with them as usual. And as usual, I took a seat on a pillow as they did but at a bit of a distance from them as a safety measure. US Marine Gen. James "Mad Dog" Mattis's words always came to me in situations like that. "Be polite, be professional, but have a plan to kill everybody you meet." And you can bet I did.

"How are you doing?" I asked.

"Good, good." I was assured with nods and more smiles. Then Ajmal produced two pieces of paper from a yellow legal tablet with words written on them in black ink. The writing was neat and very clear, but the majority of it was in Pashto, so I couldn't read what it said. I could see that the ANA was referred to several times, but only one other word was recognizable. Written in all capital English letters about seven times was a name: HERBERT.

I didn't have a clue what the letter could possibly be about or why I would be mentioned prominently by name. Looking at the pages, then back at Ajmal, I could see that he was pleased. Actually, all three of them were smiling, even, surprisingly, Delawar.

"What's this?" I asked.

"I wrote this myself, but it is a letter from all three of us," Ajmal said proudly. "It is a letter for you. It will get you elevated."

Getting me promoted, or "elevated" in their words, had been a preoccupation with the detainees ever since the first ill-fated move out of segregation. Every time they shared information, they would say something about how it could—or should, in their estimation—get me promoted. I asked Haji if he was okay with the letter, and he nodded eagerly. The three of them had a brief discussion, then Haji leaned forward and held out a hand for the pages. When I gave them to him, he signed his name on the top page in the margin, probably to put his personal stamp on it, and show that he agreed fully with the contents of the letter, whatever they were.

When the letter was given back to me, I folded it neatly, taking my time and wondering what it was all about. What could they have written? In their enthusiasm to do me a favor, had they said something that would backfire and instead paint me as a Haqqani or Taliban sympathizer? I would turn the letter over to my CW when I made my report. He would have it translated and would hopefully let me know what it said. In the meantime, I tried to look as pleased and grateful as the detainees expected me to be.

"What should we discuss today?" I asked.

Sometimes Ajmal would put the ball back in my court by saying we could talk about any topic I wanted to discuss, meaning that they were open to talking about Bergdahl. That day, however, the detainees turned the conversation toward the American and Canadian hostages they'd previously told me about.

"We were wondering, did you tell the investigators what we said about the Canadian and the American?" Ajmal asked.

"No. I don't talk to other investigators. Why?" I asked, denying any involvement with them.

"An agent came and showed us pictures of the woman. We don't know why they would think we had any knowledge of them." Ajmal translated for Haji. Then he added, "I understand the American woman has had her baby."

"She has? Is the baby okay? How is the woman doing?"

"The last we heard, they are doing fine. The father too," Ajmal told me, then caught himself. "Well, we don't know if the Canadian is the father, but he is alive and healthy as well."

That was all good news, information I filed away to be included in my report later. Right then, I was wondering if I would be able to draw more information from them about Sergeant Bergdahl's proof-of-life video.

"I was wondering about this video you told me about," I began. "If it's okay with you, you can email it to me or even arrange to have a copy of it mailed to me here on the base. Or, I don't know, maybe it would be easier to send me a link online. I could log in and see as much as you want me to. Is there a site or a link where I could see it?"

They didn't quite shut down at the mention of the video, but they made it clear that subject was off the table for the day.

"I need to talk to my brother," Haji said through Ajmal. "He will be coming home at the end of the month, no later than the first week of the new month. I will talk to him then and ask him to give you the video."

"How do you get your information?" I asked. "How will you get word to your brother?"

"My family, when they come, to talk to me on the VTC," he replied, referencing the video teleconferencing system. By using it instead of allowing face-to-face conversations, we could not only supervise their interactions with visitors but also had a video record of each exchange. "I will talk to him when he returns," he said again, indicating that the matter of the Bergdahl video was closed for now.

I still had time on the clock with Haji, Ajmal, and Delawar, so I went back to the topic of the other hostages.

"So are the American, the Canadian, and their baby being kept in a prison?" I asked. "Do you house the people you capture in places like this like the US does?" I swept my arm wide, indicating the whole of Parwan Detention Facility.

They smiled at me and shook their heads.

"No, we do not do that," Ajmal answered for the group. "We have others here, here, and here." He pointed to different spots around the room, indicating they kept their prisoners in different locations instead of in one facility. "If we want one, we may pull him from here and move him there." This time, he demonstrated by plucking a tiny invisible prisoner from one place and putting him down in another.

He may have assumed that my question stemmed from a concern that a baby would be kept in a prison because he added, "The woman did have her baby, and they are being taken care of."

Through Ajmal, Haji changed the subject back to visiting with family, but there was no more mention of the brother who could get Bergdahl's video to me. Instead, he talked about visiting with his children on VTC, saying that because they are old-fashioned, his wife doesn't communicate with him over the video system. Instead, she talks to him through the kids. Thinking of our communication methods of video chatting and texting in the states, I wondered how she would get along in America. Not well, I supposed.

Realizing I had everything I was going to get from them that day, I started to wrap up the meeting. As I reached out to shake their hands and wish them a good night, Haji said something to Ajmal, who stopped me.

"We would like to meet and talk again tomorrow," he said.

That set my radar off. Our meetings were scheduled for every other day, but I had gotten in the habit of coming to talk with them every day, whether there was an official meeting or not. They must have anticipated having additional information for me by the next day if they were going out of their way to request a meeting. I wanted to grill them and find out what they would have for me tomorrow that they couldn't tell me right then. Instead, I kept cool and said,

"Sure. I've got kind of a busy day, but I'll make time to come see you."

All three knew that I was busy and that they weren't my only responsibility, so they appreciated that I came to visit with them often. I was sure it was one of the reasons I'd remained on better than good terms with them.

After leaving the meeting room to the guard force who immediately started seating the detainees in their wheelchairs for transport back to their cells, I hunted down my CW. I would still have to prepare a written report of my interaction with the prisoners, but the letter was burning a hole in my pocket. I wanted to hand it to him personally and ask about being kept in the loop on the translation. When he saw it, he seemed interested but not troubled by it.

"I'll send it upstairs with your report. We'll see what the three stooges have to say and get back with you," he assured me.

I hoped it was all good and that it wouldn't jeopardize me or the operation.

CHAPTER 13

The next day was as busy as I'd anticipated. Between meetings, reports, and training members of the Afghan National Army, it was late afternoon before I had a chance to get over to segregation to visit the detainees. Haji clapped his hands, and an ANA guard scrambled to bring me a chair. Before sitting, I greeted them by shaking their fingers, as one finger is all they could fit between the squares of the steel mesh over the windows on their cell doors.

"How are you all doing?" I asked, taking a seat.

"Fine, fine," Ajmal answered for everyone. I turned to Haji.

"How is your leg?" I asked. He'd been feeling unwell after the hunger strike, and I knew it would please him that I remembered.

"Much better now, thank you for your concern," he told me through Ajmal.

"So you said you wanted to meet today—" I began, opening the door for them.

"Wait," Ajmal said, holding up a hand. "We want to discuss the letter we gave you yesterday. Did it please your bosses?"

"Well, I don't read Pashto, so I'm not sure what it said, but I know my superiors are going to have it translated," I told him. He smiled and nodded.

"Ah, they will be happy with it," he said, then turned the subject to the business of the day. "So what topic are you interested in?"

They had been the ones to request the meeting, but I knew this was part of the game. They wanted me to ask about the video.

"Why don't you tell me more about this video," I said. "I'm sure it would help get you moved sooner if we could get it. It would show you are cooperating, and it would cement your comfort for the rest of your days here. Getting that video will act like a lock on your future." I pointed to the lock on the door of one of their cells to demonstrate.

"Yes, yes, we would give you the video right away if we were not in here," Ajmal responded. "You must understand. We are detainees. We know the video exists, but we do not have it. We have to talk to the boss and ask him to send it."

"Your boss? I thought you said you would talk to your brother about it when he comes back in a few days."

"Yes, my brother, Jalaluddin, the big boss," Haji said through Ajmal. "He or my nephew, Sirajuddin, will have the video. They will deliver it."

As close as Haji was to Jalaluddin, it wasn't surprising that he called him a brother, rather than a brother-in-law. Something didn't sound right to me though. I doubted the leader of the Haqqani Network would come to a US military base to talk to his "brother" on VTC.

"How will you talk to him? He'll come and visit with you over VTC?" I asked. Haji shook his head and waved a hand.

"No, no," Ajmal answered for him. "We will need to call him."

"How do you plan on calling him?"

All three of them looked at me expectantly, indicating that I was supposed to fill in that blank. That was the red flag I had been expecting for months. I'd been wondering when they would ask me to bring them a cell phone. Instead of offering one, I posed another question.

"Do you have a phone number to call?"

Ajmal told me there were several numbers. As he rattled them off, I scribbled them down on my note pad.

"The phones in the district are not always good, so if no one answers at one number, we call another one," he explained. "Someone will certainly answer at one of them."

I stared at my notes, my mind racing. I doubted the guys on any level who had previously interviewed Haji had gotten phone numbers for the leader of the Haqqani Network.

"Of course, I have no control over my brother," Ajmal translated for Haji. "If I were out, it would be no problem, but it may take some time to get the video. But remember, when a letter was requested to let the family know that the sergeant was alive, that was provided. That was proof of life!"

It was true. The men holding Bergdahl had apparently allowed him to dictate a letter in his own words so the family would know it was authentic, and they'd mailed it through the Red Cross. I'd seen the report about it on CNN. But that was then and this was now and I was determined to do what I could to help find and free the sergeant.

"The family appreciated getting the letter and knowing that he is still alive, but I'm sure it would be more comforting to see him on a video. To see with their own eyes that he is doing okay."

Haji shrugged. He could only make the request.

"I will beg my brother to give you the video, but I will have to call him to do that," Ajmal translated for him.

I didn't like being backed into a corner and was determined that this wouldn't be a deal breaker.

"I have a work phone," I said casually. "I could probably arrange for you to use it, if you make it fast. But what if I called? Could I call the big boss and go meet him to get the video?"

That amused them as I knew it would.

"Would you do that?" Ajmal asked as the other two chuckled. I laughed too, back on even ground with them.

"All I want is to help people. I helped you, and you, and you from starving yourselves to death," I said, pointing first to Haji, then to Delawar, and finally to Ajmal. "If I can bring the sergeant home, then that's what I want to do."

The three nodded, approving of what I'd said. The discussion abruptly turned to large world politics then. Haji laughed as he repeated something he'd said before.

"We should be in charge, you and I. We could do it much better together."

When his watch began beeping, our meeting was over. It was time for their prayers, so I apologized for taking so much of their time and said goodnight.

On my way to grab some dinner, I thought about the prisoner's motivation for requesting the extra meeting. They'd proven that they could get messages out and receive information back. I wondered if they'd already sent word out or maybe had received the word to stall me. On the other hand, their first concern was the letter they'd given me the day before. Maybe there was something in it, and they'd wanted to know that I knew what it said. Changing direction, I decided to visit my CW before eating.

"Any progress on translating that letter?" I asked when I found him.

"Getting it word-for-word entirely is going to take some time. Not much longer, but we have the gist of what it says," he told me. I nodded for him to go on.

"At the start, the letter states that Haji, Ajmal, and Delawar have been in segregation for over nine months, and they claim to not know why they've been locked up, let alone in seg. They talk about demanding answers from both the ANA and the American government and resorting to a hunger strike after being told by both sides that they were under the other side's authority.

"Mostly, the rest of the letter is one of appreciation for 'Herbert.' They say how much they appreciate all you've done for them, and that they feel you work with them well. In requesting a transfer to a shared cell, they promise to abide by behavior standards we've set down. Essentially, they like you and agree to behave for you, and would like to work with you as their liaison for the military, both the US guard force and the ANA."

Not what I'd expected, but then again, I hadn't known what to expect. It didn't sound like the letter contained anything damning for me, but it also didn't have any clues or revelations about Bergdahl. I thanked the CW and left to find some dinner. The pace at which things were moving was already frustrating, and I wondered, not for the first time, if Haji was playing a game with me. Did the video really exist? If it did, could he actually get it to me? What if the video turned up, and it legitimately was of Bowe Bergdahl? Would there be enough on it for our guys to track down his whereabouts? For that matter, would he still be anywhere near the place where the video had been made?

I exhaled a mirthless chuckle. It was stressful enough working and living in a war zone. Working so closely with prisoners from the other side, not knowing how much of what they said could be trusted, only added to the tension and anxiety. Realizing I wasn't hungry, I changed course for the second time that night. What I really needed was a good, hard workout in the weight room.

CHAPTER 14

Although I was supposed to have a scheduled meeting with the detainees the following day, work with COIN and the ANA got in the way. An incident occurred in the detainees' communal showers, and although it wasn't hunger strike related, my CW felt I could be useful in diffusing the situation.

Requesting a move wasn't uniquely Haji's idea. Other detainees in segregation and the general population frequently asked to get transferred to a different cell for almost any reason you could imagine. They didn't get along with their current cellmates. They wanted to be in a smaller cell with fewer people. They just wanted a change of scenery. That day, two detainees who had requested several times to be moved to a different cell had refused to leave the showers when it was time to go back to their cell.

An ANA soldier whom I knew as Omar met me at the door to the shower room shaking his head.

"These guys, they're causing a big problem. I was just going to call the extraction team to remove them. I don't know what else we can do."

I'd worked with Omar before in the TA2 program. He was great at following orders, but like most of the Afghani military, he wasn't much of a problem solver.

"Did you get a chance to speak with them, or are they not talking?" I asked.

"For an hour I tried talking to them!" Omar exclaimed in frustration. "Maybe you can help. They surely won't listen to me."

I agreed to give it a shot, wanting to at least try before resorting to forcibly removing them. First, though, I needed to see if a translator was available. After checking in with the US guard force, two of them returned with me—one to act as an interpreter and the second one to provide backup, if necessary—and the four of us approached the open doorway leading to the showers. On my advice, Omar tried talking with the detainees inside again. When one of them shouted back in Pashto, he turned back to me, looking defeated.

"They say they will not talk to me," he said.

"Give it another try," I replied. "Ask them how they are doing, if they're okay. Then ask them why they won't go back to their cell."

"You are better at this, you should do it," Omar said. "You talk to them. I'll watch you and learn."

Omar knew as well as anyone at Bagram my reputation for being able to talk almost anyone out of a rebellious act, so it was reasonable to imagine that he truly wanted to gain some training from the scenario. I'd anticipated as much. That was the reason I'd brought a translator with me, to take Omar out of the equation if the detainees continued to refuse to deal with him. I nodded to the interpreter, and we stepped forward.

"This is MA1 Herbert with US OPS," I told them through the interpreter. "Are you guys okay in there?"

"We are fine, but we will not go back to cell seven," one of them responded in Pashto.

After hearing the translation, I asked, "Why not? Why won't you return to your assigned cell?"

"We cannot live in there. We have asked over and over to be moved. No one will listen, so now we will stay here until we can be in a different cell."

"You know it's not that easy to move people around in here," I said. "Most of the cells are full, so moving you probably means moving others to make room for you somewhere else."

"That is not the reason we've been kept in cell seven. Our requests are being ignored. If you force us to go back into that cell, we will cause a big disturbance. Someone will get hurt."

I turned away from the shower room, back to Omar and the other member of the guard force.

"Go over to cell seven and find out if any of these three guys is a cell leader or a mullah. Also ask if there are any issues with them, together or individually," I told the guard. To Omar, I said, "Since these guys communicated a threat, we have cause to put them in segregation. I need you to go find out if there is room over there to house them."

When the guard returned, he told me that one of the detainees in the shower room had been a cell leader, but that he had resigned. None of them was a mullah, and there had been no issues with them either. Omar came back soon too, reporting that there was plenty of room to take them to segregation. All we needed were the orders to put them there. The translator and I resumed our conversation with the detainees.

"You guys can't live in the shower room. You said if you were forced to go back to cell seven, 'someone would get hurt.' That is a threat and grounds to put you in segregation, so that is what we're going to do. We've already checked, and there are three cells waiting for you."

That had the effect I was hoping for. After a frantic whispered conversation, the designated leader called out that they would be peaceful and cause no more issues for me.

"You were disobedient to refuse to go back to your cell, and you made it worse by communicating a threat," I advised them. "You wanted to be moved, so you'll be moved—but you're going to segregation."

"That is not necessary," the detainee argued back, a pleading and placating tone in his voice that I didn't need a translator to understand. "We will follow your order to leave the shower peacefully and will cause you no more trouble."

It was the result I'd wanted, but I couldn't ignore the threat they'd made.

"You can take this from here," I told Omar. "You need to get a movement order to have them placed in seg. I'll follow up later to make sure everything is done."

In the past, I'd seen instances where obtaining the orders and assembling the personnel to get a move by force done had taken days to accomplish. Estimating that the follow-up would keep me busy for the rest of the day and probably longer than that, I knew I wouldn't have time to meet with Haji, Ajmal, and Delawar as planned. I only had a few minutes to stop by segregation to let them know I needed to reschedule, but that I would arrange for a meeting in a classroom within a day or two, once things in other areas of my life settled down. Ajmal had told me on more than one occasion that although they knew they would see me every other day, they started to wonder about me on the days I didn't visit. They would wonder where I was, what I was doing, and if I was okay. Although they said they trusted me on a level they hadn't trusted anyone else, there was still an element of insecurity because of how others had treated them in the past. If all I had was a spare a minute or two to check on them, it was worth it to maintain the connection.

It was a good thing I'd postponed my talk with Haji and the others. When I checked back on the detainees in the shower room a couple of hours later, they were still there, and no orders to move them had materialized. I immediately went to ANA OPS to talk with the US lieutenant working there with the Afghan guard force.

"What's with the guys in the shower?" I inquired. "They were supposed to get moved to seg hours ago."

"We're still working on the movement order," Lieutenant Prince advised. "There's still a problem though. They told the ANA guard force that they don't want to leave the shower and refuse to go to seg after we get the order." He pointed to two ANA guards seated at desks across the room.

A different translator than the one I'd worked with earlier was on shift by then. I asked him to tell the ANA men that the detainees in the shower had communicated a threat to me, and that left us no choice but to move them to segregation. I could tell by the tone of voice used by the man who answered that he disagreed with me, even before the interpreter translated his reply.

"That is not so. We did not hear any of them make threats."

"You tell him that it was earlier, before he came to work," I instructed the translator, mindful of keeping my voice calm. "The three detainees were speaking directly to me and in no uncertain terms communicated a threat. You tell *him* to remind them of the conversation they had with me and to get them moved."

After hearing my response, the ANA guards got up from their seats and left the room. Lieutenant Prince, the translator, and I all followed them to the shower room. There was a brief conversation between the Afghani guards and the detainees which the interpreter reported in a low voice for the benefit of those of us who didn't speak Pashto. In the end, the detainees admitted that they had threatened to incite a riot and went reluctantly but without incident to the cells that had been prepared for them in segregation.

The next step would have been to call in the extraction team, so it was a relief that the detainees backed down and seated themselves in wheelchairs for the trip without being forcibly placed in them. I didn't get the full story on why they'd wanted to be moved out of cell number seven, but they were so adamant that it was likely that they didn't get along with some of the other guys they were housed with. That episode ate up an entire day for me. Between catching up on work placed on the back burner so I could deal with it and preparing the report on it, the meeting with Haji and the others had to be pushed back more than a day, just as I'd anticipated. Soon, however, we were back in the classroom, seated on pillows and rugs and drinking chai.

All three of the prisoners had been amused with the casual aspect of our encounters ever since I'd started moving them out of segregation for our visits. At least once every other time, Ajmal would remind me that they were unshackled and would ask, "How do you like sitting here with us, unchained in this room?"

When he brought it up that day, I replied with a smile, "I'm aware that you don't have chains on. I'm not scared. I would use one of you as a weapon if needed."

They all laughed, and Ajmal again opened up the official discussion by asking about the letter they'd given me.

"Have your bosses read the letter? Have they elevated you?" he inquired.

"No, they won't promote me. The things you said in it were nice. They were good, but I won't get a promotion out of it."

That seemed to only mildly disappoint them. This time, Haji was the one to bring up the topic of the video through Ajmal.

"I asked for the movie," he said, referring to the proof-of-life video, "and it should be nothing. Since the letter was delivered to the sergeant's family, and it is already known that he is okay, it should be nothing for the movie to be sent."

I didn't question him on how he'd placed his request. Regardless of what kind of security we had, it was well known that messages could get in and out of the facility.

"I was wondering though, what about the girl?" he continued, referencing Caitlan Coleman. "What if we get a letter from her and email it to you?"

"That would be good. I could take that right up the chain to the boss. It would stimulate some talks about those kidnapped for sure," I said. I wanted to sound grateful for their willingness to help, but I also wanted to get back on the topic of the sergeant.

"Do you think Sirajuddin would meet with me to hand off the video of the sergeant or letter from the girl so that we could talk, like you and I do?" I asked.

Haji looked skeptical as he related his answer to Ajmal for me.

"The US has placed a five-million-dollar reward for the big boss, so that is not good."

"Could they send the video through several people?" I suggested. "Could they send it to someone to send it to someone, then send it to someone else whom I could meet near Kabul to collect the letter or video? Could you guarantee my safety if we did it that way?"

With the CIA and the US Army behind me, I was fully willing to meet someone from the Taliban or Haqqani Network if Haji said it was possible. He considered my idea as Delawar stroked his beard thoughtfully, characteristically silent. Then he nodded.

"Yes, that could be done, but your people would arrest him, or intelligence will play tricks. They need not arrest him. It is no good to just send people who are just trying to talk to get arrested. Then the US would win. We need assurance that no arrest will happen. Can you do that?"

I nodded confidently. My thoughts weren't on the five-million-dollar reward. I wasn't eligible to collect it doing my job anyway. However, I would promise them whatever I had to if it meant getting my hands on the video, the letter, or both.

"For something like that, I sure would!"

Haji spoke again, and when Ajmal translated, I wasn't surprised that they were changing the subject to the move out of segregation.

"Where will you be placing us? When will we be moved back to our cell together?"

"The cell I put you in before is being used now. There are other people in it. I have to find a different one. But don't worry. We'll get you moved soon."

"But where are you looking for a cell, and what day will you move us?" he pressed. "You said to wait until the general was gone, and he is gone as of today."

I'd temporarily forgotten how easy it was for these three to get information, but what they said was true. The 636th had left that very day. The previous few days had been spent in military tradition with the outgoing unit giving their replacements the rundown on what was happening and who they were dealing with.

"Very knowledgeable and true," I admitted, then altered the facts a little to buy more time. "But they are not done yet, another brigade hasn't come in, so the general can still advise and have a say on what happens. Don't worry about that though. I'll get you moved now that he's gone."

"When will you be going home?" Ajmal asked then. Among the information they'd accessed was that I would be leaving soon too. My deployment was almost over, and they were concerned that no matter what my intentions were, they might never get moved out of segregation if it didn't happen before I left. Plus, as preoccupied as they were with getting me promoted, they also wanted to make sure that the proof-of-life video was provided while I was still in Afghanistan. When I told them that I wasn't going home for a while, Haji nodded and took a moment to consider, then responded through Ajmal, "We will get you something either on the thirtieth or the first of the month. That should be in plenty of time before you leave."

"If you're talking on my behalf and asking for the letter or video for me, why don't I call your brother on the phone? I could assure him that the information is going to benefit the family that he has here"—I gestured to the three detainees—"as well as the family he has at the detention facility in the US."

Whether Haji was truly considering my suggestion or not, at least he appeared to give it some thought.

"Sirajuddin does ask why it is us requesting the video," he said. "He wonders why the United States doesn't ask for it themselves. We will talk. Maybe that is a good idea for you to call my nephew."

It was obvious that the detainees had already communicated about the video with someone on the outside by the time they told me about it. Now it sounded like they had been in touch with their bosses about it all along, even though Jalaluddin Haqqani was supposedly out of town and unreachable. It made me wonder if the video was ready and waiting for me somewhere while Haji and his boys were stalling, trying to time the handing over of the video with their move to a shared cell and my upcoming departure. All part of the game.

"An interrogator has been coming in every Wednesday and asking us about the girl," Ajmal said, suddenly changing the subject again. To them, another person asking about information they'd shared with me was a tip-off that I was passing on everything we spoke about.

"All the information you have provided to me I've held close to my chest. I am not going to give it to anyone until I can get you moved," I told him. "First things first. *You guys* are my priority."

That seemed to surprise all of them. They knew I had to pass on the information I got from them to my government. I had to keep my spin on it though, a technique I'd brought with me from working in narcotics in my civilian job as a police officer. In civilian law enforcement, whenever we deal with a confidential informant, we make it our policy to never divulge information outside of our unit. That keeps leaks under control. Letting the detainees believe I was holding information back as a way to get them moved helped me maintain my rapport with them.

"I want you to have something more," Ajmal said for Haji.

"Do you want me to give the information out?"

"Yes, if it helps you. If it elevates your position!"

I shook my head to let them know it was doubtful anything they said would get me promoted.

"It's getting late, and I've taken up enough of your time," I told them, taking a turn at changing topics.

"We have enjoyed our talk," Ajmal said on behalf of his friends. "We would like to continue to talk together in this way, but in the future, we can talk in our cell. When we are in one together, we can talk about more things."

"I'll bring the chai and the muffins as a housewarming gift," I told him, and he laughed.

All that time, not only that day but during every discussion we'd ever had, Delawar had never said a word. He'd gone from ignoring my existence to giving me cold, hate-filled stares. Then after I'd moved them temporarily out of segregation, his demeanor had changed. He hadn't suddenly become chatty, but he would usually spend the meetings stroking his beard contemplatively, nodding in agreement once in a while. Lately, he'd even smiled at me once or twice and had taken to waving in greeting when I came in the room or passed by his cell. He would also give a thumbs-up to show he agreed with whatever Haji was saying or to indicate he was doing okay. It was a little unnerving and scary to see Delawar being nice. It made me wonder if something was up, so before wrapping things up that day, I decided to bring him into the conversation.

"How is your friend doing?" I asked Ajmal, nodding at Delawar. "Why?"

"He has asked for nothing and given me no trouble. I try to make sure you all have what you need, but I've never asked if there's anything he wants, if he's doing all right."

Ajmal smiled and said, "We talk every day when we're in our cells. He is your friend as well as we are. We are looking forward to being in a cell together so that we can talk together, face-to-face, about these things."

Considering Delawar was the most intimidating out of the three, it was good to know that I was apparently on his good side. Before I left, I told Ajmal I was having a much-needed day off the next day, but that our regularly scheduled meeting the day after that would happen as planned.

"Enjoy your time then. We will be waiting for you when you come back. Hopefully, it will be the day of the move, but you are working on this," he said in parting.

It made me laugh. Now that the 636th was gone, and I would be leaving, there was no way they would let me forget about moving them.

I'd always suspected that the general and others up the chain of command knew exactly what I was doing, even though the first move had been reversed. They'd chosen to allow me to do what I did with the intention of seeing how far I could get. Having a new battalion in place that was in the process of getting up to speed would give me some time to work on the move immediately. I wasn't willing to give up my time off to do it though. It felt like I'd been working around the clock for the past several months. I'd been looking forward to an actual day off for a long time. Of course, that didn't keep me from thinking about the problem while I was off duty, and I decided to see if Agent Siaperas had any great ideas. It had become procedure to talk to him after every meeting with the prisoners. After filling him in on the status of the video and speculating that it could already be on its way, I brought up the topic of the move.

"So the three detainees are pushing more and more to get out of segregation. They know the 636th MP is gone, so I can't fall back on that anymore, and I think they're getting worried about me leaving," I said.

"That won't be immediately though, right?"

"No, not in the next few weeks, but I'm thinking if there is any way that this really is going to happen, can we make it happen now?"

"Is there a vacant cell that could be used?"

I told him about the cell I'd located. It was close to the US intel office, and it had numerous security cameras already set up nearby. Siaperas thought for a moment.

"You can tell the US personnel that we're interested in the case," he said, giving me permission to use his involvement as an excuse. "If the ANA asks, tell them that the detainees wanted to return to a shared cell."

"Roger that. I can put that information out tonight and follow up on it when I return to duty day after tomorrow," I said.

The calm, even tone of my voice hid how ecstatic I was to have a plan for moving Haji and his boys. Essentially, the strategy was the same one I'd used before: tell one side one thing while telling the other side another. This time though, Siaperas had my back, and that made all the difference in the world. Having some oversight in this game was absolutely necessary. It provided me with authoritative backup, people who could meet with those who had to be answered to and do the talking for me.

CHAPTER 15

The meetings with Haji, Ajmal, and Delawar began to run together. I lost track of how many times I talked with them, and most times, I would walk away with little to no new information. More than once, I thought we were done, that we'd hit a dead end, but now, reading back over my reports along with emails to and from everyone from my CW on up, it's easier to see that progress was being made. Haji had been telling me he would ask about getting the proof-of-life video of the sergeant around the end of the month, but barely two weeks later, I received an email from Agent Siaperas letting me know that a video had been delivered to the Bergdahl family.

That came as a surprise at first, but truthfully, I'd wondered all along if the video was already on its way. The way Haji talked about it, saying they would provide it soon, had made me think that they knew it was in transit. Of course, I thought it would be on its way to me so that I could be the one to give it to Agent Siaperas at the Strategic Briefing Center, but in retrospect, I should have known better about that too. Haji and Ajmal had acted as if they would actually consider setting up a meeting for someone to hand the video over to me, but it all came down to a matter of trust. I completely understood that. I wouldn't trust me in that situation either. Anyone they would send to deliver the video would be arrested and detained. The Haqqani Network wouldn't sacrifice their men, and it was no doubt difficult to find someone to be the mule who wasn't connected to them or the Taliban in some way and of interest to the military. Apparently, they had decided to make arrangements to have the video sent directly to the sergeant's family through the Red Cross.

I would have liked to ask Siaperas what was in the video and if it was obvious where it had been shot. In fact, what I would have liked to do was to take it in and watch it with Haji, have him narrate it for me. Other than the landscape right around Bagram, I don't know what Afghanistan looks like, and I've always thought it would be interesting to have Haji and Ajmal sitting there telling me what kind of tree that is on the side of the screen and where it grows, and whether the video was being shot in a village or at a safe house somewhere. Not that they would have given away much, but it would have been an experience for sure. I did ask for a copy specifically for that purpose, but was told, "No, the family has it." I knew other agencies had to have a copy that they were studying in minute detail. If not, there was no way I believed that they couldn't get one, but no one was going to let me see any copies, and it's my understanding that the video still hasn't been released to anyone outside of the US government.

The next time I met with the detainees after that, not one of them brought up the video. As usual, our visit started out with small talk, me asking how they all were and if they needed anything and Haji asking after my family. Then Ajmal told me they would be happy to talk about anything I wanted to. Not sure if he was trying to open the door to talk about the video, I decided to see.

"Well, I'm sure you know the proof-of-life video has been delivered to the sergeant's family," I began. Haji's eyes lit up, and Ajmal's response matched his surprise.

"No, no. We did not know it had been delivered, but we are glad to hear this. Now you know that we will do what we say we will do, just as you have."

"Yes, this proves that as well as the fact that Sergeant Bergdahl is still alive, at least at the time the video was made, so thank you for that."

"This could have been done years ago, if anyone in the US had been willing to work with us," Haji said, reiterating his appreciation for the short-lived move I'd orchestrated.

"What about the letter?" Ajmal asked, looking at the chest patch on my uniform and seeing that my rank had not changed. "The letter we wrote did not get you elevated?"

"No. No promotion yet," I chuckled. "Promotions take time, but I told you, it's really hard to get promoted over here. I appreciate the letter, but it's not going to do anything to elevate me."

"And what about the information on the woman and the baby? That wasn't valuable?"

"Oh, no, that information was very valuable," I protested. They already knew that I'd passed on the news about Caitlan, Joshua, and their baby. We'd reached an unspoken agreement not to embarrass each other with weak denials over the ultimate purpose of our meetings. Ajmal, Haji, and Delawar liked me and trusted me to a point, but they knew I wasn't visiting them out of simple friendship.

"Everyone was relieved to find out that she and the baby are fine and that the father is okay too. It's just that it's not going to get me promoted either."

"Do they need proof that what we've said is true?" Haji asked in Pashto, and Ajmal repeated in English.

"What do you mean?"

"We've already talked about getting a letter from the girl. We can have it sent, or maybe have her email her family to tell them she is all right, and the baby is healthy as well."

"That would be great. Something like that would help your cause more than it would mine," I said. Ajmal immediately understood where I was going with that remark.

"Have you found a place for us? Will you move us soon?" he asked.

I hadn't told the prisoners anything about having located a new cell for them or having official/unofficial backing on the plan to move them. It would take a little time to get the memos I needed to make the move happen, so I'd been holding that information, waiting until they asked again.

"I do have a new cell for you, and even though I don't have an exact date, I have the right people on board to make it happen. It's just a matter of getting the paperwork into place, and we'll get you outta segregation."

All three were obviously pleased with that news. Haji looked at me thoughtfully for a moment, then spoke.

"You have already done more than anyone else. We give you information, we've provided the video proving the sergeant is still alive, none of it has improved your position."

"Yes, he's alive, but he's still a prisoner. If I could get him released, *that* would be something that would get noticed," I said, intending to sound as if I were joking but hoping it would lead somewhere.

Haji still looked thoughtful.

"There were already talks about releasing him," Ajmal translated for him. "The United States didn't want him released enough to agree to the conditions."

I smirked.

"The conditions were hardly fair. The Taliban wanted twenty-four guys released for just one of ours," I pointed out. Haji shrugged, but Ajmal answered on his own.

"That's the way it is. You don't give the side holding the cards what they want. They will not give you what you want."

Trying not to show exasperation with his comeback, I asked, "Well, other than not giving up twenty-four Taliban, what do they want from the US that they can't give?"

Haji looked me in the eye and held up four fingers as he spoke three short words.

"Four for one," Ajmal translated.

He had to be kidding. Haji may have held a high rank in the Haqqani Network, but I doubted he had the authority to negotiate the release of Bowe Bergdahl, let alone suddenly drop the required number of Taliban released from twenty-four down to four. I smiled an easy cynical grin.

"Four for one? Really? That's great. Much better than twenty-four for one."

Haji nodded, and Ajmal answered.

"Yes, four men for the sergeant."

It was my turn to look thoughtful.

"Sgt. Bowe Bergdahl. You're saying that now, instead of releasing twenty-four Taliban guys, you only want four released in exchange for Sgt. Bowe Bergdahl?"

"Yes, four for Bergdahl," Ajmal confirmed. "Four for *you*. That gets you promoted."

I had to laugh at that. Even if Haji were in a position to make that offer, it wouldn't get me promoted, but that had never been the motivation for me anyway. Being elevated was their thing. All along, I'd simply wanted to be in on bringing one of our guys home. That was the payoff for me. Sitting in that classroom with those three, I wasn't sure what to believe, but it would all go in my report. If anyone up the chain of command in the military thought this offer should be taken seriously, they'd probably take over from here.

"I'm not even going to ask how you know that now, all of a sudden, the Taliban is willing to negotiate Sergeant Bergdahl's freedom in exchange for four of their men," I said, unable to hide my skepticism. "Do you happen to know the names of the four guys they want released?"

"We do," Ajmal said. He turned to Haji, who reeled off four names that meant nothing to me. To be fair though, it had always been hard for me to understand him when he attempted English, let alone when he was speaking Pashto.

"Okay, if this is legitimate, maybe we can strike a deal," I told them, nodding but still doubtful.

Later, when I verbally reported to Agent Siaperas, the news interested him, but he sounded as dubious as I was.

"Really? Four for one? Did they have names?"

"Yeah, I guess so. Haji prattled off some names I didn't really understand."

"Well, let's see if you can get them to commit to anything then. Let's get something in writing and see where it leads. How soon will you be talking to them again?"

When I told him the next meeting was scheduled in two days, he suggested I call on them the following day. It was evening before I was able to make it over to segregation to see them again, but naturally, the detainees were happy to have an unscheduled visit.

"It is good to see you again so soon," Ajmal said affably. "How are you doing today?"

"I'm doing well, and how are you guys?" I asked, anxious to get on with business.

"We are well too. Is there something you'd like to talk about?"

There was no doubt that they fully expected this extra meeting, and I was glad they seemed to want as much as I did to get right to the point.

"Yesterday you said that the Taliban would be open to releasing the sergeant if we would release four of their men in exchange. Is that true? Do you have the authority to make that offer?" I asked.

"The Haqqanis work closely with the Taliban," Ajmal told me, translating Haji's answer. "We know that the sergeant is still alive and that they are willing to trade him for prisoners your government has."

Looking at one and then another, holding each of their gazes for a moment, I remained silent, trying to determine if this was legitimate or just a game.

"What the hell," I finally said, turning to a new page in my notebook. "Can you tell me those names again? Go slower this time."

Haji nodded to Ajmal who turned to me and held out his hand, gesturing for my pen and pad of paper. Stunned, I passed them over to him. He took his time writing out the names in English letters as well as in Arabic. I took my time reviewing the list:

1. Mulla Mohammad Fazl
2. Mullah Norullah Nori
3. Khair Ulla Said Wali Khairkhwa
4. Mohammad Nabi Matii
5. Abdul Haq Wasiq

Looking up at Haji, I said, "There are five names here. I thought you said four for one."

He didn't admit to a mistake or a change of heart. Instead, Ajmal simply replied, "These are the names of the men we want in trade for the sergeant."

I looked over the list again, this time recognizing that they were all Gitmo detainees.

"These guys are all from Guantanamo," I said, speaking directly to Haji. "If you were going to add anyone extra, why not one from Parwan?"

He looked at me, questioning, waiting for me to continue.

"What about you? If I were going to make up a shortlist of detainees to release in exchange for the sergeant, I would put you on there. I would get you released so you and I could do business later on."

Haji seemed pleased that I was concerned about getting him released. He stroked his beard, appearing to think about it. Remembering that when I talked to one of the three, I was talking to all of them, I amended my list further. Pointing to Haji first, then Ajmal and Delawar in turn, I said, "I would want you out, you out, and you out. Not these five."

He smiled but brushed my suggestion aside. Through Ajmal, he said, "The United States will never let me go, but the sergeant is valuable to them. If they want him back, they will release these five men."

"Why just these five though?" I pressed. "I thought that they wanted twenty-four released before. Now they'll be happy with only five?"

The demeanor in all three prisoners changed then. It was like a switch had been flipped. Reminded of the deadlocked negotiations, they began complaining about trying to deal with the US.

"The United States," Ajmal scoffed. "They don't pay attention, and they lie."

Haji said something that had the effect of reining in Ajmal's scorn. He caught himself and looked at me in chastised apology, and I assumed Haji didn't want me insulted with a tirade against my government. Ajmal continued in a more measured tone, though his anger was thinly veiled.

"We offer money, and they pretend to consider it, then say no! We want to talk trades, they say no! It is all lies. This is our final compromise. These five men for the sergeant."

Still not sure whether this could be a legitimate offer or not, I had to act as if it was, all the while wondering if it could even happen. After all, the United States doesn't negotiate with terrorists.

"Well, that is generous, and probably more doable than twenty-four for one. I'll send this up the chain and see what they say."

Right then, Haji's watch started beeping. Glancing at it, he asked, "Will I have time to go to prayer?"

I prepared to leave, standing and thanking them.

"I'm sorry to have taken up so much of your time. I'll be back to talk with you soon, maybe even tomorrow."

It was difficult to get my head around three prisoners, well connected though they were, coming up with a reasonable offer for the release of Bowe Bergdahl. It was tempting to get excited about it, but Agent Siaperas's restrained reaction the previous day tempered mine. Thinking it over on the way back to my office, my instincts were to take it with a grain of salt. In the end, I decided to treat this meeting like all the others. I would report in verbally and type up an official report later detailing everything that was said, including the list of five Gitmo detainees. Then I'd wait for instructions to proceed, maybe from the CW of the intel unit but more likely from Siaperas and his agency. Whichever it would be, I was more interested than ever to see where this new twist would lead.

CHAPTER 16

After talking with the three detainees that evening, I placed a call to the CW and left a brief message on voicemail outlining the discussion we'd had. Naturally, I made sure to mention the highlight of the conversation, that Haji had confirmed that there was an official offer to free Bergdahl and that the number had been knocked down from twenty-four for one to five for one. When I checked in for duty the next morning, it was to multiple urgent emails and voicemail messages. Everyone up the chain of command was freaking out. Before I had a chance to return any calls, my phone rang again.

"I need some clarification on what you're saying," Siaperas said when I answered, skipping a greeting altogether.

"He initially said four for one, but the official list he gave me is five for one," I replied, calm and matter-of-fact.

"No way!"

"That's what he said. He said they will do five for one."

"We need something in writing. We need something from you that says five for one, names and all."

"I'm taking care of that this morning. I'll get it to you as soon as it's done."

Satisfied, Siaperas rang off to let me get to work. I began to take care of some loose ends from the day before, wanting to clear my desk before I started on the report, but the phone kept ringing. First, it was the CW, excited by the turn of events and asking when I'd have the report to him. Then it was someone from the Strategic Briefing Center, also asking if my report was on its way. I kept telling people that I was getting to it, that I'd have it done soon, sooner if I could get a break from all the phone calls. When Siaperas called for a second time an hour later, it was a struggle to control the irritation in my voice.

"What's the hurry? You guys don't usually put any pressure on me."

"This isn't just a typical report on a conversation that's been had several times before with multiple agencies," he patiently explained to me. "This report is going all the way up."

"What do you mean it's going 'all the way up?'"

"It's going to the White House, so we need it *now*," Siaperas said.

No shit! was what I said in my mind. "Yes, sir!" was what I said before hanging up and immediately pushing everything aside to begin on my report.

As I typed away, I couldn't help but think that this is where Haji, Ajmal, and Delawar had been going all along. It was what they were waiting for—*I* was what they were waiting for. I wasn't sure how long they'd been sitting on this offer, but they had to have already had the go-ahead to make it. When we'd talked, they didn't have to think about how many names they wanted in exchange for Bergdahl, nor had they had to think about which names those were. They'd simply popped off with a number and a name to go with each one. The three detainees had been interviewed by countless military and government personnel, but they'd also complained about how they were treated. I couldn't help but think that what they were waiting for was someone to be honest with them and treat them respectfully. Although I couldn't say I'd been 100 percent honest with them all the time, I had gone out of my way to avoid lying to them outright. Mostly, I tried to find the best outcome, find a way for everyone to get something they wanted.

Instead of printing out a copy of the report for everyone, I emailed it out. Siaperas didn't want to waste any more time, and everyone else involved wanted it right away too. After hitting Send, I turned back to the other tasks I'd started that morning. As my thoughts ran ahead to what the next step would be, I wondered if I would have enough time to finish what I'd started. I was supposed to be going home shortly, and I was torn. I missed Jean and the kids, but was I duty bound to put Bowe Bergdahl before my family?

Would I need to? They'd given us the names of the guys they wanted, and all indications were that five for one was acceptable to our government, but how soon could they make it happen? Would I need to be available for the exchange? It was such an emotionally charged situation. On the one hand, I wanted to stay as long as it took to see it through. On the other hand, I was homesick and wanted to say *screw it*! I decided to walk over and talk to the CW about it.

High from the good news I'd delivered, he waved me into his office when I arrived and had me take a seat.

"Just finished reading your report," he said, smiling. Then noticing I seemed more apprehensive than enthusiastic, he asked, "What's the problem, Herbert?"

"Well, this is pretty big, but the timing is shit. I'm leaving. My deployment is almost over, and I don't know what's going to happen here. I want to be here until it's done, to see that Bergdahl gets released, but my family knows I'm supposed to be coming home, and I *want* to go home. But if I go, what if something happens? If I'm here, I've got the rapport with Haji and the others to help smooth things out, but will it fall apart if there's no one here they trust?"

The CW had been there a long time. He understood exactly what I was saying. However, he also knew what was at stake.

"There's no telling how long it will take to get this entirely resolved," he said. "Do you want to stay on, not knowing whether it will be one more month or six more?"

I shook my head.

"If it was an extra one to six *weeks*, that might be different. I've been thinking about it though, and there might be a solution," I said. "Is there any way I can go home on schedule, then come back in a few weeks? Nothing is going to happen that fast, and I'll have a chance to see my family, take my kids to Disneyland, and you can fly me right back in. I'll pick up where I left off. I'll even give you another year if I can have a couple of weeks with my family."

He nodded, considering my offer, then presented another idea.

"You know, Haji responded earlier on to another interrogator, the first year he was here. You're closer with the detainee than he was, but they parted on good terms. We could run him down, find out where he is, and bring him in to fill your spot."

Having that option made me feel a little bit better about leaving before the job was done, and we decided to make the CW's idea plan B. I would go home on schedule, take my family on the vacation I'd promised, and be available to come back in a few weeks if something came up, and they needed me to negotiate with Haji. In the meantime, they would find the other guy who'd made friends with Haji and have him on standby in case something went down before I could get back.

Getting that resolved was a relief. Still, I couldn't relax completely until Bergdahl was in US custody. Over the next few days, the flag at Qatar that had been down for over two years went back up, signaling that both sides were willing to talk again. I imagined the process. Our side would tell the other side, "We understand you want five for one. We've been told five for one," and the other side would confirm that. They already knew who we wanted to get back, so we would ask them for the names of the five people they wanted released to see if it matched the list the detainees had given me. With everyone satisfied, an agreement would be made. As it happened, when it was all said and done, the five men released from Gitmo turned out to be the exact five men on the list Ajmal had written.

It wasn't likely that Bowe Bergdahl would be produced on the spot and handed over. It was going to take time to make arrangements for the Guantanamo detainees to be released, to appoint men to go to recover Bergdahl, to screen them and vet them, and to make travel arrangements. The Taliban wouldn't reveal where Sergeant Bergdahl was being held, but an exchange site would have to be chosen and agreed upon for both sides to feel some level of safety. With all of that needing to happen, I was sure I had time to go home for a visit with my family and be back in Afghanistan to help tie up loose ends if necessary. In the meantime, I intended on coming through with my final promise to Haji and the others. I had a cell for them and Siaperas's support in getting them moved. That was one thing I knew I could do before I left for home.

CHAPTER 17

The weeks after the stunning revelation that the Taliban was willing to release Bowe Bergdahl felt like living in suspended animation. After years of no open communication between the sergeant's captors and the US, the flag was back up at Qatar, and talks resumed. However, as I'd expected, all the little details that had to be arranged and agreed upon slowed the process down. That was frustrating enough, but I was also discouraged by not being kept in the loop as matters progressed.

Intellectually, because I know how the military works, it was understandable. On a personal level, however, I would have liked to at least have been kept apprised of the progress toward bringing Bergdahl home, considering I'd accomplished something the STC hadn't been able to do in the previous four-plus years. When I would ask, I would get a polite response that was light on details. "We're working on it." "These things take time." There was some consolation when Siaperas confirmed that the Taliban were willing to do the exchange exactly as Haji had offered: five for one. Once again, it looked like he was as important and connected as he'd claimed to be.

Because all my focus had been on the three prisoners and trying to sniff out information about Bowe Bergdahl, I felt like I was at loose ends in those weeks. I was still determined to make good on my vow to get the detainees moved again before I demobilized, so I shifted all my focus to that task. An empty cell on the ANA side of the facility was ready and waiting. The only thing that needed to be done was to have the cell next to it vacated. It housed one prisoner, but we wanted the cells on both sides of the one that would house

Haji, Delawar, and Ajmal to be empty to create a buffer between them and the rest of the population. Per Agent Siaperas's suggestion, I'd written up another transfer request for the detainees, leading off with the fact that his agency had an interest in the case. That memo had been submitted before the detainees dropped their prisoner-trade bombshell, so it wasn't surprising to get the go-ahead with a date set in following weeks before I was to leave for home.

Anticipating an approval, I had also already prepped the Afghan National Army to expect a move. I'd typed up a memo explaining the situation and requesting that the prisoner in the cell next to the one I'd chosen be relocated. Instead of emailing the request, I personally delivered it to the ANA general's office, wanting to underscore the importance of moving swiftly once the paperwork was in place on the US side. I was still trading on the respect and goodwill built up from impressing Dr. Ghanni as well as Haji's esteem. No one on the ANA side raised an eyebrow when I told them my three detainees wanted to be housed together and would be coming back to the Afghan side of the facility. Everything fell into place so smoothly that I was a little disappointed not to have to take advantage of Siaperas's offer to send anyone with questions to him.

It was still important that I maintain a good relationship with Haji and the others while the details of Bergdahl's exchange were being ironed out. I continued to visit them on a regular basis, but the excitement and anticipation I'd felt before had faded. I'd gotten the prize in the Cracker Jacks, and they'd used up their golden ticket. They didn't have much more to offer. In consideration of the job I'd done on the Bergdahl case, Siaperas thought it was worth a shot to try to see what we could do for the other hostages Haji had talked about.

"See if you can get them to follow up on the offer to have Caitlan send an email," he coached. "It would be a great gift for the family if they would include pictures of her and the baby."

It was a new challenge, and I locked onto it. I wondered if Haji had the authority to do a little bargaining and decided to spend the time before my departure working on getting more hostages than just Bergdahl released. So, soon after getting approval to transfer Haji, Delawar, and Ajmal, I paid them a visit.

"How are you guys doing? You ready for a move?" I inquired.

Their eyes lit up, and there were smiles all around.

"You will be moving us to a new cell together?" Ajmal asked.

"Yes, everything has been approved, and the arrangements have been made. The ANA has to relocate one guy, but you should be transferred sometime this week."

Haji beamed appreciatively, and Delawar even smiled and gave me a thumbs-up. I had to admit that I was almost as excited about it as they were. As usual, when Haji spoke, Ajmal translated.

"This is a great thing you have done for us. We gave you what you wanted, the sergeant is going to be released, but still you come to visit us."

"As long as I'm here, I want to make sure you guys are okay," I replied. "And of course I'm going see that the move goes off as planned."

That pleased them too.

"So! What shall we talk about today, then?" Ajmal asked, clapping his hands together.

"It's true that you generously gave me the information about the sergeant," I began, not wanting to discount what they'd already done, "but you also told me a little about the American and the Canadian and their baby. I've been thinking a lot about them since you first brought them up."

"Yes. They are all safe and doing well," Ajmal said. Instead of seeming to guess about their welfare, he was confident. That gave the impression that the Taliban still had all three, and my detainees were well aware of their location and condition.

"Yes, but I'd like to help my government end all this," I pressed. "Let's get the girl, the baby, the man, and the sergeant and trade them for the others, straight across."

"Yes, but if we were dealing with just you, then there would be no problem doing that. With your government, there are too many politics," Ajmal said, shaking his head to show how much they disapproved of the way the US conducted business. "They are not really interested in getting one for one. They only want the sergeant back."

"I'd still like to know that the girl is safe, that the baby is alive and healthy at least," I explained, trying to make some progress. "A picture or video of them would be great, but you also talked about getting a letter from her."

Ajmal looked at me as if I were stupid.

"Of course they are safe! We will talk to Sirajuddin. He will have her write a letter, and it could be copied and emailed," he said, moving his hands back and forth to demonstrate that they could scan the handwritten letter to be sent through email. "We could also have it brought by messenger too, though, who knows? It would be nothing to have someone meet you here or there."

Now we were on familiar ground. Talking about getting a video of Bergdahl is where we'd begun. I'd offered to meet with anyone to take delivery of the video, but the Taliban had mailed it to the family instead. This time, it was Haji bringing up the possibility of me meeting with someone from their organization. The thought was exciting, but troubling too.

"If I go, would I be safe?" I asked.

Ajmal nodded even as Haji was answering, then he translated, "For sure you will be safe. You are a brother. No one is safe in the mountains unless the Haqqanis say they are safe. We are in control of the area, and you will surely have our protection."

"Then I will go if the Haqqanis will get the girl's letter from the Taliban," I told them.

Seeing Haji glance at his watch, I looked at my own. It was nearly time for their prayers, but I had one more piece of business to take care of.

"I have taken up too much of your time, and you will want to pray soon," I said, signaling to the guard force. "You said that your sleeping mats were flat and worn out, so I wanted to get new ones for you before the move."

The guards brought in three new mats and proceeded to swap them out for the old ones. Naturally, that made them happy.

"If you want, we can meet tomorrow," Ajmal said as I was saying goodbye. He was letting me know that they wanted an extra meeting, but saying "if you want" was his way of putting the ball in my court so that it would be my idea. I smiled.

"Sure," I told him. "I may not be able to come until the evening, but I will get over here as early as possible."

Siaperas was thrilled with my news that day, and he emailed back within minutes. He wrote,

> Good stuff, Herbert. I received the news that the transfer was approved, and it sounds like the detainees are ready to go. When they first started talking about emailing a letter from the girl—wow. This is so much broader than what we imagined. There's no great rush to get a video though. If they get it, great. If not, that's okay. We understand these things take time. On a personal note though, as a father, I wonder about the health of the girl and the baby…do they need anything? Has the child gotten the appropriate shots or vaccinations? What about the girl? Is she getting follow-up treatment? I guess if Haji knows those answers, it would be good to find out.

He signed off by reminding me that he was going on a short leave soon.

When the detainees had first brought up Caitlan's little family being held hostage, I was interested but focused more on Bergdahl. Now that he was all but a done deal, it was starting to look like this would be the next project everyone up the chain of command would expect me to take on. I was torn, wondering how much I could get done before I left for home. It would be a challenge to try to get three more people released or, at least, negotiate an agreement for their freedom, but I was up for the task. I'd wanted something to fill the remaining time I had left. Between making sure Haji and the others got moved and working with them to get more information on the three additional hostages, I imagined I'd be pretty busy.

The meeting with the prisoners the next day would supply another opportunity to try to find out more about Caitlan and her baby. I grabbed a small notepad and flipped to a clean page. I needed to make a shopping list and started jotting down a few things I knew Haji liked. I planned to stop by the commissary before visiting them to grab a box of tea, some honey packets, and a package of cookies to grease the wheels and see if it would prompt them to share any more information.

CHAPTER 18

About a week later, Agent Siaperas sent an email informing me that he wanted to be in on my next meeting with Haji, Ajmal, and Delawar. It was unclear why he wanted to be included when previously he had no problem with me talking to the detainees and reporting on the conversations. The only thing I could come up with was that my rapport with Haji had been underestimated. No one up the chain of command had expected me to actually get a hold of information as important and remarkable as I had, so all I could guess was that they didn't want to be on the sidelines if I was able to pull it off again. Since Agent Siaperas and I were on good terms, I didn't mind waiting for him to arrive on base before going to see the three prisoners. I had a busy day ahead of me and wouldn't be able to break away before the afternoon anyway.

It was after fifteen hundred hours when I received word that Siaperas's chopper had landed. As I walked over to meet him, I wondered if he would want to take the lead in the discussion when we met with the prisoners. I supposed he would or, at the least, might leave me in charge but lay down specific instructions for how the meeting was to go.

"MA1 Herbert," Agent Siaperas said, holding out his hand for me to shake when I met him just off the tarmac.

"How was your flight, Sir?" I asked, saluting him first before shaking his hand.

"Fine, the usual scenic trip over Afghanistan," he joked dryly. "Is there somewhere we can talk before meeting with the detainees?"

I took him to the classroom I had prepared for the occasion. Closing the door behind us for privacy, I turned and looked expectantly at the agent, giving him the chance to speak first.

"First, Haji's mentioned needing to contact his 'brother' or 'nephew' to get information or instructions, so we're going to assist with that if he brings it up again."

I nodded, still curious about his presence at this particular meeting.

"So will you be questioning the detainees today, or are you just here to sit in?" I asked.

"It's going to be more of a team effort than anything," he said, producing a sheet of paper from his pocket which he unfolded and held up.

"This is a list of questions the agency wants asked. We're definitely interested in Caitlan Coleman and her baby. Joshua Boyle too. We want to get right to the point with Haji. Maybe find out what he knows about those three and how long he's known it. While we're at it, I'd like to know how long he'd been sitting on the Bergdahl information and why he decided to spill it to you."

He glanced at the page he held, then leaned forward to hand it to me. I scanned it, seeing that most of the bulleted points covered questions I'd asked in the past, though worded differently.

"One more thing," Siaperas said when I looked up from the list of questions. "You're scheduled to go home soon, likely before anything is finalized with Bergdahl. It's my understanding that there are a couple of options on the table for keeping these guys cooperative."

"Yeah, I really don't want to leave before we get Sergeant Bergdahl back," I said.

"You could always stay on longer, just until this is settled," he suggested.

"Well, it's been a long time, and my family is expecting me back. If I knew for sure how much longer I'd be here, that would be no problem. As it is, I've decided to go home for two weeks and come back if I'm needed. I can get a by-name request to return if there are any loose ends to tie up. In the meantime, another interrogator has been located, Sergeant Whitaker. Haji responded to him in the past, so the plan is to bring him in if I can't make it."

Siaperas nodded, taking the information in.

"Good enough then. Let's bring these guys in and see what we can find out."

A few guys from the guard force retrieved Haji, Delawar, and Ajmal from their cells in segregation in the usual way, wheeling them into the room, then removing their goggles. Once they were settled on pillows arranged in the corner, I gave Haji the tea and other treats I'd brought him before introducing Agent Siaperas.

"This is someone I've been working with, someone who's interested in the girl and her baby," I told them. They looked at him skeptically, but the fact that I seemed to trust him influenced them to give him a chance.

"We understand you can get a proof-of-life letter from the American girl," he said.

Haji cut his eyes over to look at me, then back to Siaperas. Although he'd spoken to me directly in halting English from time to time, he now responded in Pashto, forcing Ajmal to translate.

"Yes, we can ask for a letter from her to show that she is safe and doing well."

"There was talk about getting an email, but it would definitely have to be a handwritten letter. Do you know where she's being held?" Haji thought for a moment before responding.

"Before I can request a letter, I'll have to contact my family," he said, referring to the Haqqanis. "We'll need to find out who has responsibility for these hostages. Once we know that, we can ask for a letter and relay the information about the conditions you have for it."

Siaperas nodded.

"How are you going to contact your family?" I asked.

"It will take time, but the fastest way would be to call," Haji said through Ajmal.

"Could we make the calls for you? Using the numbers you gave me?"

"You could call," Haji allowed, "but the family would respond better, faster if I could make the calls."

The request for access to a phone didn't surprise me, and apparently, it didn't surprise Agent Siaperas either. He responded before I could.

"We appreciate your cooperation with MA1 Herbert," Siaperas offered, trying to keep the tone of the meeting positive. "The information you've provided about the girl and her baby as well as Sergeant Bergdahl is valuable."

This brought a genuine smile to Haji's face.

"Herbert has done things for us that no one else has," Haji replied.

"Is that why you've been willing to work with him when you wouldn't talk with any of the other people sent to interview you?"

Ajmal had a ready answer for that and didn't wait for Haji's response.

"The others were all stingy, foul-mouthed, inhospitable louts," he spat scornfully. "They would come to interrogate us, not to talk. They never tried to do anything for us, never brought us anything. They already had opinions about us and were hostile, treating us no better than dogs. They would accuse. 'You did this!' or 'You did that!' It didn't matter what we said. When I would deny their accusations 'No, I didn't do that!'—they would come back and insist 'Yes, you did!' The arguments would go around in circles. Would you cooperate with people like that?"

Siaperas could see his point, and it illustrated perfectly why my approach had been successful.

"Not all of them were bad," I reminded Haji. "We located the first man you worked with."

That news was well-received. Haji's eyes lit up, and he said, "Whitaker?"

"Yes, Sergeant Whitaker will be returning soon."

"He must come to visit us in our new cell. I would like the opportunity to say hello and to talk with him," Ajmal translated the words his friend spoke excitedly in Pashto.

"I'll pass on the message then," I told him.

At that point, Haji's watch alarm beeped, reminding him it was time for prayers. Siaperas knew about the watch and that it was a gift from me for helping out with keeping the houses calm and orderly.

"Looks like it's time for your prayers. We'll get you back to your cells then," I said, rising from my seat to signal the guard force to come in.

The detainees said a polite goodbye to both Agent Siaperas and me before climbing into their wheelchairs for the return ride. After they were gone, Siaperas said, "Well, that didn't go exactly the way I thought it would. We only asked a few of the questions, and we didn't give them the email address, but it was still productive."

"Are you going to arrange for a phone?" I asked.

"Yeah, but it's going to take some time. I'll try to get something lined up in the next day or two."

I nodded. Something about the meeting felt off, like we hadn't accomplished the original purpose, and I wasn't thinking about the email address.

"What?" Siaperas asked, noticing my silence.

"The meeting today was their idea," I said, pointing to the door. "I wonder if trying to get access to a phone was why they wanted a special, unscheduled meeting."

"Could be, I guess," he shrugged. "It didn't seem like they held back information or avoided any topics just because I was here."

He was right. When I thought about it, Haji and Ajmal were as talkative as they were when I met with them alone, and Delawar was as silent.

"Yeah, maybe. Or it could just be they wanted some company."

Siaperas looked at me thoughtfully.

"The approach you've taken with them is what works. After you're gone, whoever deals with them, whether it's Sergeant Whitaker or someone else, will get a lot further by treating them the way you do."

"I've documented my approach," I said. "I've pointed out how much more receptive they all are to open dialogue rather than one-sided accusations. Just bringing them a pizza or something from Burger King goes a long way with these guys. Everyone has their own style. I'm sure Whitaker realizes that, but who knows what other people down the line will do?"

Siaperas got up from his seat and began gathering papers together. He stacked them on top of a tablet of paper he'd jotted a few notes on.

"I better get to work on that phone line," he said.

I stood up too.

"Thanks for all you've done, today and over the past few months."

"Whatever I can do to help," I said.

CHAPTER 19

When approval to move Haji, Ajmal, and Delawar came, the word was that it could take time to prepare everything. That's why it was surprising one day not long after to receive an email instructing me to have the detainees ready to be transported by the following day at 1500 hours. Thinking it was news they'd want to hear immediately, I went to segregation to tell the three prisoners to get packed. When I arrived, however, I found Haji lying on his mat and Ajmal and Delawar looking concerned.

"What's going on?" I asked.

"He is sick," Ajmal told me, pointing in the direction of Haji's cell.

Haji didn't respond verbally when I looked in on him and asked what was wrong. He only shook his head and waved me away.

"This isn't good, guys. I came to tell you that you're supposed to be moved tomorrow, but the transfer could be delayed if Haji is sick," I quietly told Ajmal. It wouldn't help anything if Haji thought he might ruin their chances of moving.

"He told the guards he only wanted tea," Ajmal said gravely.

"Well, we've got another twenty-four hours. Maybe he'll be better by then," I said, fingers crossed.

One day didn't make a difference though, at least not a positive one. By the time I checked in on him the morning of the move, Haji was still unwell. Delawar and Ajmal were as worried about the effect Haji's illness would have on the move as they were about Haji himself. I was concerned too but for different reasons. If his illness was serious, if he had cancer or was dying, how would that affect what I was trying to do? If he died, who would I deal with? Would things turn out the way they were headed now, or would everything fall apart?

"Don't worry," I told them, trying to appear confident. "I'll think of something so the move can go off as planned."

Before canceling anything, I thought I'd run an idea past the CW. I didn't think there was any reason to postpone moving the two healthy prisoners and wanted to ask about sending Haji to medical first before putting him in with his friends. Fortunately, he agreed but reminded me that even the slightest change in plans required paperwork.

"The memo to the ANA will have to be changed to transfer two of them to the cell that's been prepared, and another memo will have to be written up sending the other one to medical."

I nodded in agreement but didn't waste time talking about pushing the memos through the chain of command for approval. All I'd have to do would be to type up a couple of memorandums and deliver them personally.

Glancing at my watch, I saw that I had less than thirty minutes to get it all done before the ANA guard force were supposed to start relocating the three detainees. I composed a medical transfer memo in my head as I rushed to my desk. The other memo, the one authorizing the transfer of three prisoners to a specific cell on the ANA side of the facility, was saved on my computer, and all that one needed was a little editing. Although I worked quickly, I still missed the deadline. I arrived in segregation to find the ANA guard force already there and stumped over Haji's condition.

"Slight change of plans," I told them, rushing in, waving the new orders.

"We'll be moving this one to medical"—I pointed to Haji—"and the other two will be moved as previously planned."

As before, no one questioned the orders to move them. Four of the guards got busy getting Delawar and Ajmal into wheelchairs. The detainees had gathered their few belongings and stacked them in neat little piles by their cell doors. Opening Haji's cell, I found he'd made a good attempt to get packed too.

"These guys are going to take you to medical for a couple of days," I told him. "You have all your stuff together?"

He nodded weakly. In his heavy accent, he asked, "I will go to the cell with the others when I'm better?"

"Of course! I didn't make all these arrangements to leave you in segregation."

Once the individual cells had been vacated, and the prisoners moved out, guards would come back to retrieve their belongings and deliver them to the new cell.

"Everything you have in that stack there will be waiting for you in your new cell when you're feeling better," I told Haji.

Relief flooded his pale face, and I left to make sure they could accommodate Haji in medical.

Trying to push through the move had taken up most of my day. That meant the rest of the afternoon, as well as a couple of hours into the evening, were spent on paperwork and other things that had to be kept up on until I demobilized in a few weeks. It was one of the busier days I'd had since coming to Bagram Air Base, but I still wanted to check in on Haji before I knocked off for the day.

He was dozing at first, but he opened his eyes when I spoke.

"How are you feeling this evening?" I asked.

He still didn't look good, but I hoped that the staff had been able to get him to eat something. As an answer, Haji shook his head weakly. I summoned the medic on duty to find out more.

"How's this guy doing? Has he eaten anything?"

"It looks like he was given some broth," the medic replied, glancing at the papers he held in his hand.

"And he hasn't had anything since?"

"Doesn't appear that he has."

I turned back to Haji.

"Have you eaten anything?" I asked. He shook his head.

"The doctor gave you medicine though?" I persisted.

"Yes, and I'm not as sick as before," he said in his broken English.

"Good, good. Do you think you could drink a little bit of Ensure? You need the vitamins and calories."

Haji didn't look thrilled about the prospect, but he agreed to try to drink a little. The medic brought in a can, popped the top, and handed it to Haji, who tentatively took a sip. Then he took another small drink.

"That's great. You work on that one. Not all at once though. Take it slow. I'll have this guy bring you another one in a few hours," I told him, pointing to the medic who nodded his agreement.

At least Haji was making a little progress. If he could get a few Ensures in his stomach, I could get him out of medical and into the cell with his friends.

"You'll be in with Delawar and Ajmal in no time," I said. "As a matter of fact, I was just headed over to check on them."

"Herbert, wait," Haji held up his hand. "Do you have books for me?"

Again I was surprised at how easily he got information. Only a few days before, I had received a message from another prisoner in segregation that he had two books for Haji. He wanted me to give them to him before he was moved. Of course, the books had to be examined before I could pass them on, but I'd already given them to my master chief. Provided the books didn't contain anything subversive, Haji could have them when he was transferred to his new cell.

"I'll have those books for you when you get better," I told him.

With Haji resting and as comfortably as possible, I went to see Ajmal and Delawar before calling it a night. The ANA guard force had barely delivered their belongings from segregation, and they were busy making a home out of their new cell. They planned on waiting for Haji before arranging anything, but they wanted to go through their things and pull out the items they would need in the next few hours. Delawar didn't stop working but gave a thumbs-up when I appeared at the cell door. Ajmal came over to talk.

"What do you think?" I asked, already seeing the answer in his broad smile.

"It is nice. It is good that we will be together," he replied. "What about Haji though? How is he? When will he join us?"

"He's doing much better. I'm hoping he can be moved in here tomorrow."

Delawar looked up from his small pile of things and smiled. The news pleased them both. It was obvious, however, that Ajmal wanted to get back to his task. They wouldn't talk "business" with me without Haji present, so hanging around any longer would be a waste of time.

"You guys have a good night in your new home," I said. "I'll come again tomorrow."

The next morning, I learned that Haji had drunk a few more Ensures and was doing much better. By late afternoon, he was finally in the new cell with his buddies. It was a busy day for me, and although I made sure I was on hand for his move from medical, I didn't have time for a regular meeting. The prisoners didn't seem to mind. Now that they were all back together, they were going to be occupied getting situated in their new home.

I waited at the door as the guard force wheeled Haji in and removed his goggles. After the guards locked the cell door behind them and left, I looked in. A crisp new plastic shower curtain had been provided, and Haji immediately got to work helping Ajmal hang it. It was kind of cute if not a bit surreal to see these three terrorists being so domestic.

"I gotta get going, guys," I said.

Ajmal stopped what he was doing and came to the door.

"You will come back to talk?" he asked.

"Yeah, of course I will. We're not finished doing business," I said with a smile.

"Come whenever you have time. Wake us up if you have to. That is no problem."

"Well, we'll try to get back to our regular schedule of meeting every other day. Maybe I can come back day after tomorrow."

He nodded his approval and went back to helping Haji with the shower curtain. Before I could leave, Delawar surprised me by coming over to the door. Although he'd warmed up to me over the past few months, he'd never approached or spoken directly to me. Now, he carefully but clearly said, "Thanks, man. Thanks, man!"

"You bet. It's what I do," I told him, stepping back to go.

"Thank you, Herbert," Ajmal and Haji called after me as I left.

CHAPTER 20

Transferring Haji, Ajmal, and Delawar to a shared cell essentially marked the end of my time in Afghanistan. There were a couple of weeks left before I would be going home, so there was still time for me to accomplish something more. Although the Taliban had officially agreed to trade Sergeant Bergdahl for five of their men from Gitmo, the process was painfully slow. I'd anticipated that, but it was still frustrating to see my mobilization coming to an end and realizing that business probably wouldn't be finished.

That left the matter of Caitlan Coleman, Joshua Boyle, and their baby, which I was happy to work on while I was still on hand to help. After I'd reported in on getting the three detainees settled in their new cell, however, I received orders to stop pursuing any line of questioning about them.

Things are becoming more sensitive now.

That was how an email from Agent Siaperas began.

We need you to stop asking about proof of life, letters, etc. Talk about *other* topics, continue to cultivate the relationship.

So I was to continue to meet with the prisoners on a regular schedule until I left, but I was not to discuss the other hostages they'd told me about. The command blindsided and baffled me. After the job I'd done with Bergdahl's case, I couldn't imagine why Siaperas and others up the chain of command wouldn't want to take advantage of the trust I'd built up with Haji and get as much information as they could about other hostages while I was still at Parwan. Maybe strike a deal as well for the safe return of more captives in addition to Bowe Bergdahl. On the other hand, knowing that the government clearly had good hardworking people on the case, they didn't owe me an explanation. With those instructions in place, I would do what they asked, still keeping my ears open so anything of interest or value I heard from the detainees could be reported.

After the intense weeks of my world revolving around the next meeting with Haji and the others and anticipating what new information they might divulge, it was a letdown to simply visit them for the sake of a visit. They didn't have anything else to share about the sergeant and apparently didn't possess any information on other subjects that they hadn't already given me. Our meetings quickly fell into a predictable pattern, with even the topics of conversation usually going down the same unsurprising path.

I would enter the hallway that ran in front of their cell, and Haji would clap his hands twice, signaling the Afghani guard to fetch me a chair, just as he had done when he was still living in segregation. Whatever they'd been doing before my arrival, all three would stop and greet me and ask about my health. Then they would invariably ask if I'd been "elevated" yet.

"Why would I be promoted?" I responded during a meeting soon after they'd met Agent Siaperas. Haji's answer was a bit surprising.

"The sergeant will be released soon, but we've also made the phone call to the family. These things should elevate you in the military," Ajmal translated.

Until Ajmal told me, I hadn't known that Haji had made a call to the Haqqani family. Although it was tempting to pump him for details about the phone call, I had to restrain myself and follow orders. Instead of questioning him about the hostages, I said, "Those are very valuable things, but why would they elevate me?"

When Haji spoke, his tone revealed as much as his words that he felt he'd done me a great personal favor. Through Ajmal, he said, "Because you moved us and helped us, we have done these requests for you. From within our cell walls, we provided information first about the sergeant, then about the girl. Your government wants this information. They want to know about the boy and the girl. Getting that information should make you look good to your bosses. They should elevate you for the work you've done."

"Yes, that information is getting me a lot of attention, but it's getting you a lot of attention too. Your cooperation made it easier for me to get you moved to this cell," I told them. Then I added, "I may get recognized, but only after we get the missing people back."

All three nodded, accepting my explanation for the moment, but they would ask about my status again before my demobilization. Their momentary silence gave me the opportunity to change the subject.

"So how are you guys doing in your new home?" I asked, waving a hand at their spacious new cell. The three of them hesitated, looking at each other before Ajmal answered.

"It is good we are together at last," he began, wanting to make sure I knew that they were grateful I'd kept my word to move them. "There are some difficulties though. It was very quiet when we were in segregation, but it is much louder here."

"Yes, there are many more detainees here, and your cells aren't very far from other ones that are full of people." I nodded, knowing that sometimes prisoners in the larger cells remained awake all night talking, moving around, and otherwise making noise. "I can see that would be hard to adjust to, but I'm sure you'll get used to it in time."

"We are missing things too," Ajmal went on. "Haji lost his watch, and I'm worried more things will be taken away from us, like our T-shirts and lotion and other things you've given us."

That wasn't much of a surprise. I had provided memos that should have allowed the detainees to keep the items that would otherwise be considered contraband, but it was typical that the ANA guard force would use the move as an excuse to "misplace" memos and possessions.

"Don't worry about that," I reassured them. "I will take care of getting Haji's watch back and will provide new memos so you'll be able to keep your lotion and other things."

All three noticeably relaxed at that news. Then Delawar spoke the most words I'd heard him utter during my entire time at the detention facility. I tried to hide my shock and looked to Ajmal for the translation.

"He says that he owes you, and he wants you to eat with us," Ajmal said, smiling as he spoke.

From what I'd picked up about the culture, I knew what a big deal that was, and the invitation was all the more significant coming from Delawar. He had once ignored my existence and now wanted to share a meal with me. The complete change was amazing and disturbing at the same time. I was immediately on guard, wondering what they were planning and if they would finally make a move against me during the meal. Rather than committing to eating with them, I simply smiled at Delawar and nodded.

As usual, I continued to report to my CW on my daily visits with the prisoners. Since they'd been the ones to bring up the subject of Caitlan and her baby, I used that to try to get permission to pursue the subject again. I explained that the detainees had always been kind of obsessed with getting me promoted and that they'd mentioned having made a call to find the American woman's whereabouts to facilitate a request to have her write a proof-of-life letter.

Are we still standing by on questions?

I wrote this at the end of the CW report.

I will be talking with them again soon, so if you have any suggestions on questions I should ask, let me know.

The response email was polite and encouraging but carried the message that I was to continue avoiding the subject.

MA1, thanks. You are doing great work— something that really helps the good guys. I'm pleased to hear it and, having gotten to know you, am not at all surprised at the impact you're having. It's also not surprising that the detainees are concerned about you getting proper recognition for your part in all of this. It's important to remember that recognition to Afghans is extremely significant. I suggest you steer the conversation toward the possibility of the "elevation," as they put it, and away from the hostages. Tell them you are sure you'll get recognized, but it will take time. Maybe even throw in that you are only doing what you think is the right thing. That you just want to help them and don't want the recognition. Humility is always a useful card to play…

As my departure date drew nearer, many meetings with Haji, Delawar, and Ajmal were postponed, rescheduled, and sometimes canceled. A new unit had arrived to replace the one I'd come with, so in addition to typical everyday business, we also had to train the new guys to take our places in other aspects of assigned jobs. I didn't know it at the time, but I would only have two more meetings with the detainees.

When there was just a week of my tour left, I stopped by their cell to find Ajmal gone. Because he was the interpreter, the task of speaking with me fell on Haji, the only other one of the three who could speak some English. When he saw me at the cell door, he smiled and came over to greet me.

"Herbert! How are you today? What is going on?"

"I thought I'd stop by to check on you guys. I've been busy training, but I got your watch back from the guard force," I said, handing it to him through the bars of his cell.

"That is very, very good!" he exclaimed, beaming. "Thank you, thank you!"

"I've secured that with a memo," I told him, pointing to the watch. "Actually, I wrote a memo for all three of you, securing all your personal items. The guard force won't be able to take your books, lotions, watches, or anything else anymore." I showed him the memos I'd be putting in the official binder for the guard force to reference.

"Ah, that is good," Haji replied, strapping the watch to his wrist.

"So where is Ajmal?" I asked, looking around the cell.

"He is gone to a cell leader meeting," he told me in his thick accent. Although he understood English well and could get his ideas across, it was difficult for him to carry on a full conversation. He preferred having Ajmal translate for him.

"If you want to talk longer, you should come back later, when Ajmal returns," he said.

"I might not be able to make it back over today, but I'll try to come again tomorrow or sometime in the next few days."

That answer seemed to satisfy him. We said goodbye, and Delawar smiled and waved as I left. Now that they had what they wanted, they weren't as concerned about keeping my attention and requesting meetings. They'd settled into a comfortable routine and were happy to go about their business. All three had made it clear that they were grateful to me, but once they'd given up all the information they had, they knew that their existence at Parwan Detention Facility was as good as it was going to get.

CHAPTER 21

When my final day at Bagram arrived, one of the priorities on my list of things to do was visit Haji, Ajmal, and Delawar one last time. Once they'd been moved, we had stopped meeting in classrooms. One reason was that the schedule had become so irregular that it didn't make sense to have a room prepared if things were going to be rescheduled. However, the detainees were happy and comfortable in their new cell. Since they were all together and not separated by walls, they didn't mind much that bars and a cell door stood between us as we talked.

As usual, the prisoners were well-informed on what was going on at the base and knew that this would be the final time we met. When I arrived, they came to greet me. Although they all wore smiles, there was an air of sadness about them.

"How are you today, Herbert?" Haji asked. "Your health is well?"

"Yes, thank you, I am fine. How are you guys doing today?"

"We are all well, thank you," Ajmal replied for the group. As we settled in for one last time, I realized that other than Delawar's attitude toward me, nothing had changed with the three of them since our first meeting. Ajmal did most of the talking—and did all of the talking in English. Haji sat and listened, interjecting information and opinions in Pashto from time to time for Ajmal to translate. Delawar paced around the cell, his hands clasped behind his back as he listened to the conversation.

"Will you have tea with us?" Ajmal asked.

"Sure. Thank you," I replied.

They already had things prepared, including a plate of cookies they'd made themselves. When Ajmal offered them to me with a cup of chai, I picked one up, surprised.

"Where did you get these?"

"We made them here, right in our cell," he said, obviously proud of their ingenuity. "We mix powdered milk with sugar and spread it out on a plate, then let it dry for a couple of days."

Considering they spent most of their time praying or sleeping, at least they used part of the rest of their days on productive activities such as figuring out how to make the most of their small environment, rather than plotting riots, escapes, or more hunger strikes.

"We are glad to see you, Herbert," Ajmal told me. "We know you will be leaving tomorrow and wondered if your bosses told you to stop coming in and talking to us."

"Oh, no, that's not the case. Things have been very busy with training people and getting ready to leave. The time got away from me," I explained.

"We have not had a chance to talk in a while, so we have not gone any further in getting information about the kidnapped people. Now that you are going, should we continue to ask questions? To learn about the girl and her baby?" Ajmal asked.

"Yes, that is still important information," I encouraged. "Her family will want to know she is alive and safe. They would probably want to know about the baby too. Anything you can do to help would be great."

"From what we know, she and her baby are fine. The Canadian man too. They are being taken care of and treated well."

I hoped that was the case, but because I was leaving and couldn't follow up on any of it, I wanted to encourage them to do unto others as I'd done unto them.

"If I have taught you anything, I hope it is that you should take care of the people you are holding the same way I have taken care of you. I know they are being taken care of now because you need them, but what happens after they are no longer needed?"

Haji supplied the answer to that question.

"No harm will come to them. A reporter from the New York Times was kidnapped some time ago, and he was later released. He wrote an article about how the Haqqanis took such good care of him. You can look it up as confirmation."

Later, I did do just that and found not only the one article Haji referenced but a five-part piece written by David Rohde. He reports for the *Times*, but in 2008, he was visiting Afghanistan doing research for a book he was writing. Roughly two weeks after arriving in the country, he was kidnapped along with two Afghani men working with him. In the article, Rohde writes that his Afghani colleagues were treated worse than he was, with their captors almost constantly threatening to kill them when they weren't scolding and criticizing them for cooperating with a foreign journalist. Rohde, however, was indeed treated well during his time as a hostage. He says he was given water, allowed access to an outdoor courtyard, and never beaten during his time as a hostage and that his captors told him that Islam commands treating prisoners well, a mandate they vowed to follow. Initially, I had to take Haji's word that the American, the Canadian, and their child would be treated well, but reading David Rohde's account gave a bit more hope.

"So what will happen with us, now that you're leaving?" Ajmal asked, abruptly changing the subject. "Will our health be looked after? What about the cases the American government has made against us?"

"Medical and criminal issues are confidential, very secretive," I replied. "I can't really tell you anything I haven't already and wouldn't be able to assist in finding information I don't have access to."

"Will we be left here together, or could we get moved again?"

"Well, I no longer have control over moves, but I don't know why you would be separated or put into another cell at this point."

"We are worried a little to be left in the hands of the Afghan National Army," Ajmal said, his voice dropping to a confidential tone. "The Afghani general told us that everyone would be moved to another house on the ANA side of the prison and that some releases would be completed."

"Releases? Will you be getting released?" I asked. It wouldn't be surprising for the ANA to release any of these guys if the Haqqani family came up with the money.

"No, the US has made me a big dog," Ajmal replied, shaking his head. "It will cost more than thirty-five thousand dollars for me to be released now."

Haji spoke then, and I waited for Ajmal to translate.

"There is a man in another cell on this side of the prison. He used to drive for Haji. He received ten, ten, and ten years," Ajmal said, flashing the fingers of both hands three times. I supposed that mean the man had been sentenced to thirty years total for his involvement with Haji and the Haqqani Network. "Haji would like to arrange a visit with this man, to encourage him. Can you do this, Herbert, while you are still here?"

"Today is my last full day here," I told him. "All I can do now is forward the request. Maybe someone else can arrange it if permission is granted."

With the discussion back on my departure, it was time to wrap up the meeting. Seeing that I was preparing to go, Ajmal spoke.

"We must stay in contact," he said. "Can we email you?"

"Sure, I don't have a problem with that," I said, completely hiding the fact that having terrorists as pen pals wasn't very appealing. This wasn't the first time they had suggested corresponding through email. I had discussed the pros and cons of it with Agent Siaperas, acknowledging that the detainees wouldn't necessarily be friendly in a real-life environment but reasoning that if they had more information about the girl and her baby, and they preferred to give it to me rather than anyone else, I could pass it on to the right people and still be useful in getting them released. In the end, we agreed that giving them my email address would create more risk than any help it would generate.

"Once you're gone, you should avoid any direct personal contact with them," Siaperas had said. "Any information they want to pass on to any agency should only be through channels we have in place. There is an email address dedicated for receiving proof-of-life information. Using that email address provides us with options that a personal email wouldn't."

Siaperas had given me the email address to pass on if and when Haji suggested it again. Up until my last day on the base, he hadn't. Now that they were bringing it up, I would give it to them instead of my personal email. The detainees had obviously discussed keeping in touch with me through email because once I'd agreed, Ajmal immediately relayed a plan.

"You would need to use a code word so we would know that the emails are from you," he explained.

"What do you mean? I'm not following what you're saying."

Haji came up with examples for Ajmal to relate to me.

"When we email you, the first time you respond, you should write 'two Ensure' in the subject line because that is what you fed Haji to finish the hunger strike. The second time you email us, use the phrase 'shaking fingers' because we could not shake hands with you through the mesh on the door of our cell, so we only shake fingers. The third will be 'my friends in Alpha.' This will validate the three emails are from you."

It sounded like they only expected to hear from me three times. It made me wonder if they already knew what they wanted to say, and maybe that they already had the emails composed and waiting to be sent out. When Ajmal asked me for my personal email address, I gave him the one Siaperas had set up.

Finally, I stood up, ready to leave. Delawar stopped pacing and joined Ajmal and Haji at the side of the cell nearest me. Ajmal wiped at his eyes.

"I'm sorry for crying, but it's hard to say goodbye," he said, determined to show a stoic front. "You've done so much for us. I promise, one day I will find you and thank you with no cell doors to separate us, no guards standing nearby."

His declaration sounded sincere, but coming from someone affiliated with Al-Qaida, it was difficult not to hear it as a threat.

"If we stay in touch, I will encourage Haji to continue to help you," he said, patting his friend on the shoulder.

Haji and Delawar both smiled sadly as we said our final good-byes. As much as I'd kept up my guard with those three for the months I'd worked with them, it was odd to realize I was feeling a little sad too as I left the prison for the last time.

CHAPTER 22

The trip back home to the States was a blur, essentially the journey to Afghanistan run in reverse. Emotionally, I was in a weird place. Naturally, I was happy and relieved to be back with my family, but it was strange to go from being 100 percent immersed in the vital effort to find Bowe Bergdahl and help free him to doing mundane things like mowing the lawn and working my civilian job. Jean and I took the kids to Disneyland as planned during the spring break. That only took up a little over a week of my time though. After that, I returned home ready to get the call saying I was needed back in Afghanistan to finish the job I'd started. In addition to seeing the sergeant released, I also wanted to find a resolution for Caitlan and Joshua and their baby. Although everything was underway for getting Bergdahl back home when I'd left, the fact that his release hadn't been completed, as well as the situation with the other hostages, had me feeling like there were still things that needed to be done.

When a few weeks went by with no word and no orders, I called my master chief and asked her to find out if I'd missed something.

"You just got home. You want to go back already?" she asked incredulously.

"I feel like I didn't finish. I have to put this to bed so I know I did the job the best I could," I told her.

She checked it out for me, going to the lengths of polling the chain of command throughout the entire United States, but didn't come up with anything. Not only didn't she find my name on any return orders, but she also couldn't get information on the progress of Bergdahl's release.

Of course, no one back in Qatar or Bagram were going to call me and say, "What do you think? Should we release an extra guy to see if it speeds things up?" They had what they needed, so it didn't matter to anyone that I was gone. They didn't care who had talked to the detainees, who had gotten the information. It was painful to realize that I was merely a number, that I had served my purpose, and my services were no longer required. There were days when I sat in my car, wrestling with trying to put it all behind me and feeling as if I'd failed.

Did I fuck up? Could I have done anything else? Is this guy going to get out or not? The uncertainty tormented me for weeks after my return home.

One afternoon at the end of May, I was lying on the bed trying to get some rest before reporting to work for an evening shift when the phone rang.

"Are you watching TV?" I recognized my master chief's voice on the other end.

"No, should I be?"

"Yeah, turn it on. Any news station. Bergdahl has been released."

And that's how I found out that Bowe was safe and was finally coming home.

Watching the press conference in the White House Rose Garden, I stared at the words scrawling across the bottom of the screen, only registering a few of them now and again. Likewise, not much of what the president was saying made it through the fog of my shock. I remember hearing him say that we never leave our men and women in uniform behind. He said something about getting Bowe reunited with his family as soon as possible, and I recall wondering how soon that would be. When he started talking about the five Gitmo detainees who would be released in exchange for Bowe, I turned the television off.

Looking at the reflection of the room behind me in the blank screen, I reminded myself that everything had been set in motion while I was still in Afghanistan. It was all in progress and happening during my last days there and while I was on my way home as well as those past weeks while I'd been second-guessing myself. I wished that

I'd been in the information loop during that time, but it was understandable that I'd been left out. There had been many people working on getting him free for years, well before I found myself in the middle of it. From that perspective, I knew it would be impossible to decide how to let everyone involved know that his release was official when it finally happened. Who do you even tell? A lot of people involved on many levels found out watching the news, just as I had.

AFTERWORD

Sgt. Bowe Bergdahl would go on to be released later the same day of the White House Rose Garden press conference with no hitches in exchange for the five Taliban detainees. Though he was no longer a hostage, his ordeal was far from over. He would go to a military hospital to be treated for medical and emotional issues. When he returned to the US, he would learn that the military was bringing charges against him. It may still yet be a long time before Bowe Bergdahl can resume his life, and it's likely that he never will. For the rest of us, everyone else who became involved and so invested in seeing him freed, at least his release marked a point from which we could start getting on with the business of living our lives.

Part of getting on with my life has included writing this book. Not only did it help tie up the loose ends I felt remained for me, but it was also a way to acknowledge all those who have gone unthanked for their service and sacrifice in relation to this one man. What's more, it provides the opportunity to thank those who are still serving in our military protecting this great country.

Even with the frustrations I experienced, along with the lack of closure, I have always been thankful for the opportunity to have served on this mission assisting our government in the operation to bring the only American soldier POW in Afghanistan home. In total, the US Navy, the US Army, and many different agencies and services staffed with professional personnel and soldiers worked tirelessly for years on this mission because the United States never leaves a man behind.

While it took five years to bring Bowe home, this book only covers my part in the negotiations for his release and, by comparison, seems brief. So many little details had to fall into place for it all to work out as it did, and I have to thank God for the entire experience.[vii] The synchronicity and the way things unfolded, the seemingly sudden change of heart that only required we release five detainees rather than twenty-four for one of ours—all of it was too coincidental to be anything other than his will, and I am grateful to have been able to play a part in it.

NOTES

i   Psalm 40:5: "Lord my God, you have done many things—your wondrous works and your plans for us; none can compare with you. If I were to report and speak of them, they are more than can be told." All Scriptures from the CSB version unless otherwise noted.

ii   Galatians 5:22: "But the fruit of the Spirit is love, joy, peace, patience, kindness, goodness, faithfulness."

iii   Proverbs 18:16 NASB: "A man's gift makes room for him And brings him before great men."

iv   James 1:19: "Everyone should be quick to listen, slow to speak, and slow to anger."

v   1 Peter 5:8: "Be sober-minded, be **alert**. Your adversary the devil is prowling around like a roaring lion, looking for anyone he can devour" (emphasis mine).

vi   Matthew 10:19: "But when they hand you over, don't worry about how or what you are to speak. For you will be given what to say at that hour, because it isn't you speaking, but the Spirit of your Father is speaking through you."

vii   Romans 8:28: "We know that all things work together for the good of those who love God, who are called according to his purpose."

ABOUT THE AUTHOR

Randy Herbert is the author behind *24/1*. He is a Christian, combat veteran, father, husband, former narcotics detective, and native Idahoan. His experiences across military and law-enforcement communities have provided him with a plethora of narratives on the human experience. Randy has been an American-loving patriot since childhood, raised one hundred miles from where Bowe Bergdahl called it home. He continues to live in Idaho. You can usually find him in the gym, on a motorcycle, or knee-deep in a project.

CPSIA information can be obtained
at www.ICGtesting.com
Printed in the USA
LVHW030011100821
694794LV00003B/246